TRADITIONAL CHINA
IN ASIAN AND
WORLD HISTORY

Key Issues in Asian Studies, No. 9

AAS Resources for Teaching About Asia

TRADITIONAL CHINA IN ASIAN AND WORLD HISTORY

TANSEN SEN
AND
VICTOR H. MAIR

Association for Asian Studies, Inc.
825 Victors Way, Suite 310
Ann Arbor, MI 48108 USA
www.asian-studies.org

KEY ISSUES IN ASIAN STUDIES

A series edited by Lucien Ellington, University of Tennessee at Chattanooga

"Key Issues" booklets complement the Association for Asian Studies' teaching journal, *Education About Asia*—a practical teaching resource for secondary school, college, and university instructors, as well as an invaluable source of information for students, scholars, libraries, and those who have an interest in Asia.

Formed in 1941, the Association for Asian Studies (AAS)—the largest society of its kind, with close to 8,000 members worldwide—is a scholarly, non-political, non-profit professional association open to all persons interested in Asia.

For further information, please visit www.asian-studies.org

Copyright © 2012 by the Association for Asian Studies, Inc.

For orders or inquiries, please contact:
Association for Asian Studies, Inc.
825 Victors Way, Suite 310
Ann Arbor, MI 48108 USA
Tel: (734) 665-2490; Fax: (734) 665-3801
www.asian-studies.org

Library of Congress Cataloging-in-Publication Data

Sen, Tansen.

Traditional China in Asian and world history / Tansen Sen and Victor H. Mair.

p. cm. — (Key issues in Asian studies ; no. 9)

Includes bibliographical references.

ISBN 978-0-924304-65-1 (pbk.) 1. China—Civilization.
2. China—Civilization—Foreign influences. 3. China—Relations. 4. Aliens—China—History. 5. Culture diffusion—China. I. Mair, Victor H., 1943– II. Title.

DS721.S395 2012

303.48'251—dc23

2011042500

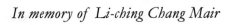

In memory of Li-ching Chang Mair

About "Key Issues in Asian Studies"

Key Issues in Asian Studies (KIAS) is a series of booklets engaging major cultural and historical themes in the Asian experience. *KIAS* booklets complement the Association for Asian Studies' teaching journal, *Education About Asia*, and serve as vital educational materials that are both accessible and affordable for classroom use.

"Key Issues" booklets tackle broad subjects or major events in an introductory but compelling style appropriate for survey courses. Although authors of the series have distinguished themselves as scholars as well as teachers, the prose style employed in *KIAS* booklets is accessible for broad audiences. This series is particularly intended for teachers and undergraduates at two- and four-year colleges as well as advanced high school students and secondary school teachers engaged in teaching Asian studies in a comparative framework and anyone with an interest in Asia.

For further information about *Key Issues in Asian Studies, Education About Asia*, or the Association for Asian Studies, visit www.asian-studies.org.

Prospective authors interested in *Key Issues in Asian Studies* or *Education About Asia* are encouraged to contact:

Lucien Ellington
University of Tennessee at Chattanooga
Tel: (423) 425-2118; Fax (423) 425-5441
E-Mail: Lucien-Ellington@utc.edu
www.asian-studies.org/EAA

"Key Issues" booklets available from AAS:

Zen Past and Present by Eric Cunningham

Japan and Imperialism, 1853–1945 by James L. Huffman

Japanese Popular Culture and Globalization by William M. Tsutsui

Global India circa 100 CE: South Asia in Early World History
 by Richard H. Davis

Caste in India by Diane Mines

Understanding East Asia's Economic "Miracles" by Zhiqun Zhu

Political Rights in Post-Mao China by Merle Goldman

Gender, Sexuality, and Body Politics in Modern Asia by Michael Peletz

About the Authors

TANSEN SEN is Associate Professor of Asian History and Religions at Baruch College, The City University of New York. Currently he is visiting senior research fellow at the Nalanda-Sriwijaya Centre, Institute of Southeast Asian Studies, Singapore. His area of research focuses on India-China interactions, Indian Ocean trade, and the Chinese community in India. He is the author of *Buddhism, Diplomacy, and Trade: The Realignment of Sino-Indian Relations, 600–1400* (University of Hawai'i Press, 2003).

VICTOR H. MAIR is Professor of Chinese Language and Literature at the University of Pennsylvania. He is a specialist on medieval vernacular Buddhist literature and, for the last two decades, has led an international team of scholars and archaeologists investigating the Bronze Age and Early Iron Age mummies of the Tarim Basin. His most recent publications are two edited books, *Secrets of the Silk Road* (Santa Ana: Bowers Museum, 2010) and, with Mark Bender, *The Columbia Anthology of Chinese Folk and Popular Literature* (New York: Columbia University Press, 2011).

CONTENTS

List of Illustrations

Maps

Figures

EDITOR'S INTRODUCTION

Tansen Sen and Victor Mair, because of their wide-ranging knowledge of traditional China, creativity, and hard work, have written a superb addition to the *Key Issues in Asian Studies* series. Overcoming the mistaken stereotype of an "isolated China" should be a high priority objective for any professor or teacher who introduces students to World or East Asian history—and this booklet will prove an excellent pedagogical tool in achieving this goal.

There are several commendable features of *Traditional China in Asian and World History* that should make it a lively as well as informative read. Although this *Key Issues* booklet will assist students in gaining a basic chronological understanding of traditional China, the authors stay focused upon the theme of Chinese interaction with other cultures and provide engaging multiple examples of it in various manifestations ranging from Chinese perceptions of foreigners to vivid descriptions of China-related regional and international commerce and the roles of religious pilgrims in fostering intercultural contacts. The authors' lucid prose is greatly enriched by eighteen maps, thirty illustrations, and three supplementary primary source readings suitable for classroom use. The utilization of this number of graphics is unprecedented since I began editing the series, but readers can be assured that each one strengthens the value of the booklet. It is difficult to imagine how the authors could have done a better job producing such a concise, yet rich, basic introduction to traditional China, and thoughtful students and instructors who read and reflect upon the booklet will most probably hereafter, if this is not presently the case, conceptualize traditional China as substantially involved in regional and world history and by no means isolated from other cultures.

Working with Tansen and Victor was certainly a pleasure and I am grateful for their openness to suggestions and persistence in crafting such a good booklet. However, this booklet would not have been possible without the work of several people. Special thanks go to Keith Knapp, who read the initial proposal for this booklet and to Jeffrey Richey and Charles Hayford, who provided excellent specific suggestions on the completed first draft manuscript. As the number of booklets in the *Key Issues* series continues to grow, I am, as always, deeply grateful to the AAS Editorial Board, AAS Publications Manager Jonathan Wilson and AAS Publications Coordinator Gudrun Patton for their strong support of pedagogy as evidenced by such projects as *Key Issues in Asian Studies* and *Education About Asia*.

Lucien Ellington
Series Editor, Key Issues in Asian Studies

Acknowledgments

We would like to thank Emily Toner for help with the preparation of maps. Patricia Martin assisted us in finding images and obtaining permission for their use. We also want to thank various institutions and presses for giving us copyright permission for illustrations, maps, and the primary sources included in the Appendix. We are grateful to Paula Roberts for help with editing and proofreading. We would also like to thank the two anonymous reviewers of the manuscript for helpful suggestions and useful comments. Above all, we wish to express our gratitude to Lucien Ellington and Jonathan Wilson for inviting us to write this volume in the first place and for guiding us through every step of the way. As *Key Issues in Asian Studies* Editor and AAS Publications Manager respectively, they were both encouraging and rigorous. If this volume succeeds in meeting the purposes for which it was intended, much of the credit should go to them.

CHRONOLOGY

ca. 500,000–300,000 years before present	Peking Man
ca. 5000–3000 BCE	Yangshao Culture
ca. 3000–2000 BCE	Longshan Culture
ca. 2200–1766 BCE	Xia dynasty (not yet historically attested)
1766–1050 BCE	Shang dynasty
1046–771 BCE	Western Zhou dynasty
771 BCE	Raid on the Western Zhou capital Haojing by a nomadic tribe
771–221 BCE	Eastern Zhou dynasty, further divided into the Spring and Autumn period (771–256 BCE) and the Warring States period (481–221 BCE) based on historical annals covering these periods
558–330 BCE	Achaemenid dynasty in Persia
551–479 BCE	Probable life span of Confucius
Sixth century BCE	Presumed dates for Laozi, the alleged founder of Daoism
Fifth century BCE	Presumed date for the Buddha in India
331 BCE	Greek king Alexander's invasion of southern Asia
ca. 320 BCE–ca. 185 CE	Mauryan empire in southern Asia
304?–232? BCE	Reign of King Ashoka in India
221 BCE	The unification of China by Qin Shihuangdi
221–206 BCE	Qin dynasty (originally established as a state under the Zhou dynasty in 897 BCE)

206 BCE–220 CE	Han dynasty, further divided into the Western Han dynasty (206 BCE–9 CE), Xin dynasty (9–23 CE), and Eastern Han dynasty (24–220 CE)
141–87 BCE	Reign of Emperor Wu (Han Wudi) of the Han dynasty
138 BCE	Zhang Qian's mission to Central Asia
57 BCE–935 CE	Silla kingdom in Korea
37 BCE–668 CE	Koguryo kingdom in Korea
ca. 27 BCE–ca. 180 CE	Pax Romana period of the Roman Empire
18 BCE–660 CE	Paekche kingdom in Korea
First-second centuries CE	Transmission of Buddhism to China
First-third centuries CE	Kushana empire in Central and South Asia
220–589	Period of disunion in China
399–416	Faxian's pilgrimage to India
ca. 450	Establishment of Nalanda University in India
589	Reunification of China by the Sui dynasty
606–47/48	Rule of King Harsha in northern India
618–907	Tang dynasty
627–45	Xuanzang's pilgrimage to India
650–705	Reign of Empress Wu Zetian in China
661–750	Umayyad caliphate, the first Islamic empire, based in Damascus
671–95	Yijing's travel to India
Seventh-thirteenth centuries	Srivijayan empire in Southeast Asia
710–94	Nara period in Japan
750–1258	Abbasid caliphate in the Persian Gulf, based in Baghdad

751	Arab army defeats the Tang army at the Battle of the Talas River in Central Asia
755–63	An Lushan rebellion
780	Implementation of the *liangshui fa* (twice-yearly tax) by the Tang court
794–1185	Heian period in Japan
ca. 850–1279	Chola kingdom in southern India
907–60	Five Dynasties period in China
907–1125	Liao dynasty of the Khitans
918–1392	Koryo dynasty in Korea
960–1279	Song dynasty, further divided into the Northern Song (960–1127) and Southern Song (1127–1279)
1038–1227	Xixia dynasty of the Tanguts
1115–1234	Jin dynasty of the Jurchens
1185–1333	Kamakura period in Japan
1205	Beginning of Genghis Khan's conquests
1256–1335	Ilkhanate kingdom of the Mongols in Persia
1271–1368	Yuan dynasty of the Mongols
1274 and 1280	Yuan naval offensives against Japan
1275–92	Marco Polo travels in China
1281	Yuan naval offensive against Champa
1293	Yuan naval offensive against Java
1336–1573	Muromachi period in Japan
1368–1644	Ming dynasty
1392–1897	Choson period in Korea
1405–33	The seven maritime voyages of Zheng He

INTRODUCTION

In recent years, scholars have successfully challenged the perception that Chinese civilization, especially in its early phase, existed in isolation with little or no influence from other regions of the world. Similarly, the passive role of Chinese dynasties in their interactions with neighboring societies, emphasized in earlier studies, also has come under serious scrutiny. Taking these recent analyses into account, this book offers a radically revised view of China's past, demonstrating the importance of cross-cultural interactions in shaping Chinese history from the earliest times to the middle of the fifteenth century. It shows how the cross-cultural linkages established by traders, missionaries, immigrants, military and diplomatic missions, and other travelers transformed Chinese society in fundamental ways. It also illustrates the important role of Chinese dynasties in cross-regional and cross-continental networks and their role in influencing societies far distant from the Central Plains, the area around the Yellow River that would later become the nucleus of China.

The first chapter outlines the value, as well as the shortcomings, of the ancient Chinese records on neighboring societies and foreign kingdoms. These records not only provide detailed accounts of cross-cultural interactions; they also offer significant insights into the Chinese perception of foreign societies and in some instances the views of foreign peoples about Chinese society. This chapter also examines early Chinese attitudes toward the role of the emperor and perceptions of China in the wider world, especially with regard to diplomatic interactions, foreign trade, and religious exchanges.

Demonstrating that the Central Plains from an early period interacted with neighboring societies and acquired foreign technologies and ideas, the second chapter explores the pre-Han period of Chinese history (i.e., before the third century BCE) in the context of the emergence of other settled societies and the movement of nomadic tribes elsewhere in Asia and the world. Knowledge of how to build chariots, and of the equestrian arts and

1

equipment, in addition to various foreign commodities, entered the Central Plains, either directly through contact with nomadic peoples or indirectly, passed on through itinerant traders and travelers. These agents were also responsible for transferring goods and ideas from the Central Plains to other regions of the world. The networks of cross-cultural interactions between the Central Plains and other settled and nomadic societies, as this chapter argues, seem to have been established long before the period usually acknowledged.

Some of these early networks developed into the so-called Silk Routes with, as explained in chapter 3, the expansion of the Han empire (206 BCE–220 CE) into Central Asia and the spread of Chinese civilization to the coastal regions. The establishment of the Seleucid (312–63 BCE), Parthian (247 BCE–224 CE), and Sasanid (224–651) empires in Persia, the formation of the Kushana state in central and southern Asia, and the Pax Romana phase of Roman history (ca. 27 BCE–ca. 180 CE) helped make interactions along these routes more secure and profitable for long-distance traders and other travelers. Indeed, travelers and traders from still more far-flung regions of the world started arriving in Han China through these conduits, bringing with them exotic goods and ideas. This chapter focuses on three aspects of the formation of the Silk Routes: the impact of Han military expansion in Central Asia on the political, economic, and cultural situation in Asia; the ways in which the demand for and export of Chinese silk linked the major markets of the Central Plains to those in the Mediterranean region; and the multiethnic nature of the transmission of Buddhist doctrines during the Han period.

The transmission of Buddhist doctrines to China was a significant event in Asian and world history. Not only did the acceptance of the doctrine drastically transform the lives of the people living in the Central Plains; it also created unique linkages among kingdoms and societies extending from present-day Iran to Japan. Chapter 4 outlines the history of China from the third through the tenth centuries within the context of the formation and expansion of these unique linkages. Issues addressed include the impact of Buddhism on Chinese society; the role of Buddhism in fostering the exchange of ideas, commodities, and diplomatic missions among various other regions of Asia; and the importance of the Buddhist-centered India-China exchanges to Asian and world history.

The final chapter charts the emergence of China as a major participant in cross-cultural commerce from the tenth to the mid-fifteenth centuries. It analyzes the changes in economic policies during the Song (960–1279), Yuan (1271–1368), and Ming (1368–1644) dynasties that influenced world trade. Foreign trade during these three dynasties was significantly different from that of previous periods: bulk goods instead of luxury items formed a major component of the materials exchanged, traders and ships from China vigorously engaged in commercial activity overseas, and the profit from overseas commerce became an integral part of state revenue. In addition to examining how the explosion of trading activity influenced Chinese society, including changes it brought to Chinese cuisine and the enhanced role of the merchant class, this chapter outlines the formation of Chinese diasporic communities in Southeast Asia and the resulting spread of Chinese culture across the Indian Ocean. The chapter ends with an analysis of the voyages of Admiral Zheng He (1371–1433) in the context of expanding global trade and the Ming court's desire to revive the traditional notion of the supremacy of Chinese civilization.

The appendix offers a selection of primary sources that underscore the theme of cross-cultural interactions between the Central Plains and the outside world. These are Chinese notices on foreign peoples and societies from before the Common Era to the fifteenth century. The selections are meant to give readers a basic understanding of the wide-ranging, complex, and often ethnocentric nature of the sources employed in writing this book.

A Note on Terminology

Two terms in this book perhaps need to be clarified. The first is *Central Plains*, which refers to the main part of the Yellow River valley, especially the area that is now Henan Province. The word *Sinitic* is sometimes used to describe things associated with "China," particularly Chinese languages and the people (the so-called Han) who speak them.

To make this volume easier to read for non-specialists, we have decided not to use diacritical marks for Sanskrit, Japanese, and other non-Sinitic terms.

1

CHINESE PERCEPTIONS OF FOREIGNERS AND FOREIGN LANDS

Archaeological and textual sources indicate frequent interactions between foreign peoples and those settled in the Chinese heartland dating to at least the Shang dynasty (ca. 1766–1050 BCE). These interactions took the form of exchanges of commodities as well as armed conflict. Perhaps the defining moment in the early history of such interactions took place in 771 BCE, when the so-called barbarians invaded and pillaged the capital of the Zhou dynasty (1046–221 BCE). Thereafter, the threat from neighboring tribes was highlighted in Chinese sources and the methods of dealing with them were articulated by various scholars, philosophers, and strategists, including the earliest Ru (Confucians, those who followed the way of the sage, Confucius), for whom Zhou culture set the standard for excellence in civilization.[1]

In the first century BCE, when Sima Qian (ca. 135–86 BCE) compiled the first Chinese dynastic history, he devoted special chapters to foreign peoples and lands. The subsequent dynastic histories continued this tradition of providing special sections, usually titled with terms that essentially signified "foreigners," "outsiders," or even "barbarians," in which the court historians offered ethnographic accounts of the foreign peoples, including their tributary relations with Chinese dynasties. These accounts usually highlighted the cultural superiority of the Chinese people and the military supremacy of the Chinese court and employed a Confucian framework in depicting the Chinese emperor as the Heaven-mandated ruler of the world. The foreign kingdoms in this context were all perceived as tributary states of the Chinese dynasty. The foreign people, who were often named with characters using Chinese radicals for various animals (especially insects and canines), were frequently depicted in these dynastic histories as uncivilized, lacking proper social norms, and submissive to the authority of the Chinese court (Yang 1968; Waley-Cohen 1999; Abramson 2008).[2]

The followers of Buddhism in China were quick to realize that the automatic description of foreigners as uncivilized and barbaric did not hold true, at least in the case of India.[3] Buddhist doctrines, as chapter 3 outlines, entered the Chinese heartland sometime in the first century CE. The religious texts and stories about the Buddha and the land in which he dwelled depicted a society that was on a par with that of the Chinese. The eyewitness accounts of India provided by Chinese pilgrims visiting the "holy land" reconfirmed to the Chinese clergy and lay followers of Buddhism in China that India was a civilized, culturally developed, and sophisticated society. In fact, some Chinese Buddhist monks argued that India should be recognized as the center of the world. Such views of India in Chinese Buddhist writings persisted until around the tenth or eleventh century (Sen 2003).

Sometime in the eleventh century, Chinese traders and merchants started to venture into foreign markets. There was a keen interest in foreign goods and commodities at the Song court, which established various customhouses at its port cities. These customhouses, through Chinese and foreign itinerant traders, started collecting material on foreign people and kingdoms, and some of these materials were compiled to form new ethnographic records of foreign lands. There were also instances in which people accompanying traders and mercantile ships wrote eyewitness accounts of foreign regions. These notices and records were significantly different from the dynastic histories described above. Unlike the Confucian worldview presented in the dynastic histories and the utopian perception of India found in Chinese Buddhist works, these works were more focused on the description of urban dwellings, flora and fauna, and goods produced and traded by the foreign kingdoms.

THE CHINESE COURT AND FOREIGN LANDS

The first Chinese dynastic history, known as *Shiji* (Records of the Grand Historian), was intended to provide a comprehensive history of China from the legendary Yellow Emperor to the Han dynasty. The compilers of the work, Sima Tan (ca. 165–110 BCE) and his son Sima Qian, worked as court scribes and had access to a vast quantity of books and documents. They were also witness to one of the most glorious periods of Chinese history under Han Emperor Wu (r. 141–87 BCE), who had expanded his empire deep into eastern Central Asia. The father and son team established a format for later court historians who were likewise charged with writing dynastic histories (essentially, the history of the preceding dynasty). The *Shiji* and these later dynastic histories consisted of several sections, of which the "annals" (biographies of Chinese emperors), "genealogies" (of the ruling family, high officials, and other eminent people), and "biographies" (of various ministers and regions) were the most important. Records of foreign regions and kingdoms appeared in the biographies section under the subheading "foreigners."

The most prominent foreign people mentioned in *Shiji* are the Xiongnu, the arch-enemies of the Western Han empire (206 BCE– 9 CE), who occupied the northern and north-western borderlands of Han China. They are

Figure 1.1. Tomb figurines of foreigners in China. (© Trustees of the British Museum.)

described as a people with no writing system and no knowledge of propriety or righteousness (Watson [1961] 1993: 129–30). The cruelty and violent nature of the Xiongnu, especially toward Han China, are depicted throughout the work. As an example, the leader of the Xiongnu, a person named Modu (his name is also spelled as Modun, Maodun, etc.), is reported to have killed his father and "executed his stepmother, his younger brother, and all the high officials of the nation who refused to take orders from him" (134). However, the laws of the kingdom are portrayed as just, even though extreme at times.

> [A]nyone who in ordinary times draws his sword a foot from the scabbard is condemned to death. Anyone convicted of theft has his property confiscated. Minor offenses are punished by flogging and major ones by death. No one is kept in jail awaiting sentence longer than ten days, and the number of imprisoned men for the whole nation does not exceed a handful. (137)

Perhaps the most interesting account in the chapter on the Xiongnu is a dialogue between a diplomatic envoy from the Han court and a Chinese eunuch named Zhonghang Yue, who had allied himself with the Xiongnu. In the dialogue, which is included in its entirety in the appendix to this volume, Zhonghang Yue rationally explains to the envoy the contemptuous perceptions the people in Han China seem to have about the social and cultural customs of the Xiongnu, including the practice of sons marrying stepmothers upon the death of the father. He also questions the Chinese pride in their emphasis on etiquette and "sense of duty," which in his opinion eventually decays and leads to enmity between rulers and the ruled. "Pooh!" he says (Watson [1961] 1993: 144), mocking the Chinese and their "civilized" ways: "You people in your mud huts—you talk too much! Enough of this blabbering and mouthing! Just because you wear hats, what does that make you?"

As described in chapter 3, the Xiongnu had a powerful army that often routed the Han forces. As a consequence, the Han court was forced to negotiate a peace agreement with the Xiongnu in exchange for large quantities of precious goods and sometimes Chinese princesses for the Xiongnu chieftain. Thus, the usual way of referring to foreign kingdoms as "vassal states" is not used for the Xiongnu in the *Shiji*. In fact, some Chinese officials were astonished that the "proper" order of the world had been reversed because the Han court had started sending gifts to a barbaric ruler.

The sovereign-vassal relationship between the Chinese dynasties and foreign kingdoms, which was symbolized by the tribute missions sent to the court in China by foreign kings, originated in the Confucian view of the wider world and the place of the Chinese ruler within this world order. Confucius and later Confucian scholars perceived China as the center of the world, calling it Zhongguo, the Middle Kingdom. The emperor of the Middle Kingdom was known as the Son of Heaven because he had acquired legitimacy through the mandate to rule from Heaven, a concept that originated during the Zhou period and was later incorporated into Confucian texts as part of the governing ideology. Within this framework, the Chinese ruler was also perceived to be the sovereign of foreign peoples and lands, especially because the latter were considered uncivilized, greedy, unruly, and barbaric.[4] Only the Chinese ruler, legitimized by Heaven, could turn them into civilized societies. Tributary missions from foreign kingdoms to the Chinese court were meant to confirm this sovereign-vassal relationship (Fairbank 1968).

With the acceptance of Confucianism as the state doctrine during the Han dynasty, the concepts of the Son of Heaven and the sovereign-vassal relationship became integrated into Chinese statecraft and foreign affairs. Most officials who served at the court, including those responsible for compiling dynastic histories, were trained in Confucian teachings. Thus, in the diplomatic exchanges and correspondence between the Chinese court and foreign kingdoms these viewpoints were repeatedly emphasized, even when the Chinese ruler had no military control over the kingdoms that sent tributary missions.

During the Three Kingdoms period (220–80), for example, the Wei court (220–65) wrote to the female ruler of Japan in the following way:

Although living far away [from China], you have sent an envoy to pay tribute. [This action shows] your loyalty and filial piety [toward me]. I am very fond of you. Now I confer upon you the title "Pro-Wei Queen." A gold seal with purple ribbon has been encased and entrusted to the governor of Daifang, who will grant it to you temporarily. [By so doing, I wish] you to rule your people in peace and to endeavor to be devoted and obedient [to me]. (Tsunoda and de Bary 1964: 16. For a study of diplomatic interactions between Chinese and Japanese rulers, see Wang 1994.)

The bestowal of honorary titles and return gifts were the usual ways in which the Chinese rulers thanked the tribute senders.

Rarely do we find the reality of the situation—that is, the Chinese ruler's lack of authority over foreign kingdoms—acknowledged at the court. One such instance took place during the Tang dynasty (618–907) when the founding ruler, Emperor Gaozu (r. 618–26) questioned whether it would be appropriate to call the Korean kingdom Koguryo (37 BCE–688 CE) a subject territory because in reality the Chinese had no control over the land. "We respect all creatures and do not wish to be haughty and superior," said the emperor. "We only occupy and possess the land, striving to bring peace to all the people. Why should we order Koguryo to be our subject in order to acquire for us greatness and honor?" One of the stunned officials replied:

It cannot be allowed [for them] not to be subject. If we allow ourselves to be put on an equal footing with Gaoli (Koguryŏ), how will the barbarians of the four directions look up to us? Moreover, the Middle Kingdom is, for the barbarians, like the sun to all the stars. There is no reason to descend from superiority to be on a level of equality with those in the barrier zone. (Pan 1997: 208)

The Tang emperor seems to have listened to the advice of his minister and maintained the traditional Confucian practice of designating the Korean kingdom a vassal state. Indeed, the solicitation of tributary missions from foreign kingdoms continued during the Song and Ming dynasties.

Tributary missions during the Song dynasty are particularly noteworthy because the dynasty had been thoroughly defeated by three of its northern neighbors, the Khitans, Tanguts, and Jurchens. The Song court was forced to sign peace treaties that required sending annual tribute to these three foreign kingdoms. It was also humiliated into recognizing the victors as political equals and sharing the symbolic Mandate of Heaven. The tribute system during the Song period, as described later in the book, focused more on the pragmatic fiscal needs of the state than on maintaining the Confucian world order. Despite this, some court officials and the dynastic history of the

9

Figure 1.2. Tribute mission. (© Trustees of the British Museum.)

Song continued to portray tributary missions as recognition that the Chinese emperor was the sovereign head of the entire world. Proper protocol and the relative status of the tributary kingdoms, as the following selection from *Songshi* (Dynastic History of the Song) indicates, remained a concern for these officials.

> In the fifth year of the *Chongning* reign period (1106) the kingdom of Pugan (present-day Myanmar/Burma) sent envoys to offer tribute. The imperial order was issued to give them the same treatment in reception as given to the envoys of the kingdom of Zhunian (Cholas, in southern India). According to the Department of State Affairs, [however,] [the kingdom of] Zhunian is subject to [that of] Sanfoqi (i.e., Srivijaya, present-day Indonesia), and therefore, during the *Xining* reign period (1068–77), the imperial edict [to it] was written on a large (plain) silk backed with white paper and kept in an [ordinary] box covered with an [ordinary] wrapping cloth. Now, Pugan is a large kingdom, and [therefore] it cannot be looked down upon as a kingdom subject to another. It is desirable to treat it [in reception] like Dashi (Arabia), Jiaozhi (present-day Vietnam) and other [kingdoms]. All the imperial edicts should be written on a silk with flower design in gold and backed with white paper, be kept in a gilt box locked with a silver key, be covered with a brocade wrapping cloth, and be sent with the envoys. This suggestion [made by the Department of State Affairs] was adopted. (slightly modified after Karashima and Sen 2009: 307)

This record is important for two other reasons. In addition to providing a description of how the Song government prepared to receive tribute missions, it also offers the court's perception of the dominant foreign powers in the region. In this case, however, the Song court's knowledge about the relationship between foreign kingdoms was inaccurate. The kingdom of Zhunian, or Chola (848–1279), in southern India, which is mentioned in the record, instead of being subject to Srivijaya (ca. 683–1288) had, in reality, defeated the latter kingdom in a fierce naval battle that took place in 1025. In fact, the Cholas, who were given the status of a small tributary state, were the most dominant power in the Indian Ocean region during the eleventh and twelfth centuries.

Despite such factual mistakes, exaggerated Confucian viewpoints, and other shortcomings, the records of foreign kingdoms in the Chinese dynastic histories offer vital information about the interactions between China and other parts of Asia and the world. Although the court scribes emphasized the superiority of the Chinese emperor vis-à-vis the foreigners, both militarily and culturally, it is evident that the relationship between the Chinese court and the foreign kingdoms was multifaceted. These records underscore the fact that these complex interactions between ancient China and the neighboring regions, as well as far-flung foreign peoples, had existed unhindered since before the Common Era.

The Holy Land of the Chinese Buddhists

The Confucian perception of barbaric foreigners was sternly challenged by Chinese Buddhists for what they considered to be mistaken views on India. Confucian (and also Daoist) adherents in China were stunned by the fact that a growing number of Chinese, including commoners, elites, and even some rulers, were following the teachings of a foreigner, reading and reciting in a foreign language, and making pilgrimages to a foreign land. Some criticized the followers of Buddhism and argued that the doctrine was meant to control the unruly foreigners and offered nothing to the civilized society of the Chinese. Others engaged in composing polemical literature attacking the Buddha and Buddhist doctrines. But, like Buddhist doctrines, the perception of India as a holy land and civilized territory penetrated Chinese society, so much so that the Confucian scribes found it difficult to portray the Indian subcontinent as just another barbaric land.

The Chinese Buddhist pilgrims who visited India and returned to China to write about their journeys were instrumental in developing the perception of India as a holy and civilized land. Their works were widely read and cited by non-Buddhist writers, including the composers of dynastic histories. The fact that the records of pilgrimages were eyewitness accounts that detailed not only the practice of Buddhism in India but also the lives of ordinary people and the sophisticated governance system employed by their rulers, made it difficult for the Confucian and Daoist critics to present a dramatically different picture of India. Failing that, the Daoists at one point tried to argue that the founder of their religion, Laozi, had gone to India to teach the Buddha or was himself transformed into the Buddha and was, thus, responsible for making India a civilized country.

Three Chinese Buddhist pilgrims and their writings played a key role in shaping (and confirming) the view of India as a civilized, cultured, and sophisticated land. These three pilgrims were Faxian (337?–422?), who visited India between 399 and 409 (and returned to China around 416); Xuanzang (600?–664), who traveled to India sometime in 627 and returned in 645; and Yijing (635–713), who went to India in 671 and returned in 695. These three were among hundreds of Chinese monks who made pilgrimages to India during the first millennium CE. And, while there were other Chinese monks who wrote about their journeys to India, no accounts are as detailed and influential as those written by Faxian, Xuanzang, and Yijing.

Faxian's record was particularly important because he was the first Chinese monk to give a detailed eyewitness account of the Buddhist holy land. Called *A Record of the Buddhist Kingdom*, Faxian's work from the outset depicts the impact of Indian culture in foreign lands. In Loulan (Kroraina), in eastern Central Asia, for example, Faxian reports seeing natives who dressed like the Chinese but followed the customs of India. The local Buddhist clergy, according to him, read Indian books and practiced speaking the Indian language. Perhaps more noteworthy, however, is the account of how one of the Chinese monks accompanying Faxian was mesmerized by Buddhist sites and monastic institutions in India. The monk, Daozheng, decided not to return to China and remarked, "From now until I attain Buddhahood, I wish that I will not be reborn in the borderland" (Legge 1965: 99–100). In other words, Daozheng, like many other Chinese monks, perceived China as the "borderland" and India as the central realm, a view that was contrary to the Confucian concept of China as the Middle Kingdom and other regions as peripheries. In fact, a sixth-century writer used one of the passages from Faxian's account to describe the region in India known as Madhyadesa (Middle Country) in the following way.

> From here to the south all [the region] is Madhyadesa. Its people are rich. The inhabitants of Madhyadesa dress and eat like people in the Middle Kingdom. (Sen 2006: 27)

Faxian and Li Daoyuan, the author of this paragraph, use the same Chinese word, *Zhongguo*, for both Madhyadesa and China, perhaps to underscore the similarities between the two regions. Indeed, in the context of Chinese discourse on foreign peoples, in which foreign eating habits and clothing were usually held up against the sophistication of Chinese culture, this statement indicates the unique status of the Indians in the Chinese world order.

Another Chinese pilgrim to be confronted with this notion of China as a borderland area was Xuanzang. In a conversation with his Indian hosts at the

Figure 1.3. Buddhist map of India based on Xuanzang's descriptions.

Nalanda Monastery just after he decided to return to Tang China, Xuanzang was reminded of the peripheral position of China in regard to the Buddhist world centered in India. "Why do you wish to leave after having come here?" inquired one of the puzzled monks at Nalanda. "China," he continued, "is a borderland where the common people are slighted and the teachings of the Buddha are despised; the Buddhas are never born in that country. As the people are narrow-minded, with deep moral impurity, saints and sages do not go there. The climate is cold and the land is full of dangerous mountains. What is there for you to be nostalgic about?" (Li 1995: 138).

Although Xuanzang defended the country he had come from as civilized, the perception of China as a peripheral and less sophisticated region was exactly the opposite of the position that the Confucian scholars and officials took with regard to China's cultural status vis-à-vis foreign lands. For them, the Indian view must have come as a shock. They were undoubtedly also astounded by the writings of a Chinese monk called Daoxuan (596–667), who in the seventh century passionately argued that India, not China, should be considered the center of the world. Daoxuan framed his argument with calculations of the distances between the geographical determinants of the mountains and seas and the two countries, as well as a comparison of the levels of cultural sophistication achieved in India and China. For example, he noted that the Indian language and literature were "divine" because they were created by the gods. The Chinese writing system, on the other hand, he pointed out, had no legitimate origins and lacked a fixed alphabet (Sen 2003: 9).

These depictions and perceptions of India among the Chinese Buddhists made the issue of the place of China in the wider world much more complicated than the Confucianists assumed. The Confucian court scribes who composed the dynastic histories ended up using accounts of India found in Buddhist writings and rarely attempted to portray India as a less sophisticated region than China, as they did with nearly all other lands outside China. Consequently, considering typical Chinese views of foreign peoples and regions, Chinese perceptions of India were unique.

CHINESE TRADERS AND FOREIGN MARKETS

By the early tenth century, foreign trade and commerce had emerged as important concerns of both the people and the courts in medieval China. This is reflected in the appearance of a new genre of Chinese writing that recorded foreign kingdoms and regions without either the Confucian or Buddhist frameworks described above. Information about overseas regions presented in these works was collected either by foreign traders arriving at the ports of China or by Chinese merchants traveling abroad. The thirteenth and fourteenth centuries witnessed the establishment of Chinese diasporic communities in parts of Southeast Asia and the founding of a vast Chinese maritime network. As a result, many of the Chinese records on foreign regions written after the tenth century deal with the maritime world.

One of the key sources for judging the Chinese perception of foreign kingdoms and peoples during this period is *Zhufan zhi* (Description of Foreign Peoples). A person named Zhao Rugua, who was charged with overseeing maritime activity in the southern Chinese port of Quanzhou, compiled this work in the twelfth century, drawing on information gathered from itinerant merchants. While the first part of the book describes forty-six foreign kingdoms and regions, the second part explains the origins of forty-three commodities that were imported by Song China. The chapters describe the main products and exports of foreign kingdoms, their economic conditions and military prowess, and the tribute missions sent to the Song court. The section dealing with foreign commodities states their place of origin and the ways in which they were produced.

The kingdom of Srivijaya in Southeast Asia and the Arab region were the most important trading partners of China during this period. Many of the commodities entering the markets in Tang and Song China originated in the Arabian Peninsula and were supplied through the ports of Srivijaya. Merchants from both these regions were active in the coastal regions of China and frequently appeared at the Song court as tribute carriers. Describing this trade between Song China and the Arab ports through Srivijaya, the work notes:

> The Dashi (or Arabs) are to the west and north (or northwest) of Quanzhou at a very great distance from it, so that foreign ships find it difficult to make the voyage there direct. After these ships have left Quanzhou they come in some forty days to Lanli, where they trade. The following year they go to sea again, when with the aid of the regular wind they take some sixty days to make the journey. The products of the country are for the most part brought to Srivijaya, where they are sold to merchants who forward them to China. (Hirth and Rockhill 1966: 114)

The author of *Zhufan zhi* was evidently confused about the founder of Islam, whom he calls "the Buddha." Describing Mecca, the Muslim holy city, he writes:

> The country of Majia is reached if one travels from the country of Maluoba (i.e., Malabar) for eighty days westward by land. This is the place where the Buddha Mohammed was born. In the House of the Buddha the walls are made of jade stone of every colour. Every year, when the anniversary of the death of the Buddha comes round, the people from all the countries of the Dashi assemble here, when they vie with each other in bringing presents of gold, silver, jewels and precious stones. Then also is the House adorned anew with silk brocade. Farther off there is the tomb of the Buddha. Continually by day and night there is at this place such a brilliant refulgence (radiance) that no one can approach it; he who does loses his sight. Whosoever in the hour of his death rubs his breast with dirt taken from this tomb, will, they say, be restored to life again by the power of the Buddha. (124–25)

The confusion between Buddha and Mohammed seems to have resulted from a misconception about the extent of Buddhist influence outside China and India, as well as a limited knowledge of Islam and other foreign religions among the Chinese scribes and officials. In fact, whenever these Chinese scribes and officials were confronted with foreign religions such as Christianity, Islam, or Manichaeism, they tended to use Buddhist terminology to describe them. In other words, the experience of virtually all alien faiths by medieval Chinese was shaped by the formative encounter between China and its first major foreign faith, Buddhism.

Information about Mecca improved significantly during the Ming period, as the document in the appendix indicates, due to the visit to the region by Admiral Zheng He. Indeed, the seven voyages of Zheng He, outlined in chapter 5, significantly added to Chinese knowledge of the maritime world. Accompanying Zheng He on the voyages were writers who kept detailed records and notes about the places the entourage visited. One such person was Ma Huan, who in 1451 composed a work titled *Yingyai shenglan* (Overall Survey of the Ocean's Shores). The book offers detailed information about the ports and kingdoms Zheng He and the accompanying officers visited. Similar to *Zhufan zhi*, *Yingyai shenglan* provides a minute account of the economic and commercial conditions in these maritime kingdoms but also includes descriptions of social conditions and customs. Writing about Hormuz, for example, Ma Huan, a Muslim, reports:

> The king of the country and the people of the country all profess the Muslim religion; they are reverent, meticulous, and sincere believers; every day they pray five times, [and] they bathe and practice abstinence. The customs are pure and honest. There are no poor families; if a family meets with misfortune resulting in poverty, everyone gives them clothes and food and capital, and relieves their distress. (Mills 1997)

As the above discussion indicates, the Chinese notion of foreign peoples and lands was diverse and multifaceted. It should, however, be noted that these sources offer only a partial view of Chinese perceptions. There were many foreigners who settled in the ports and towns of China and frequently interacted with the Chinese. Foreign Buddhist monks traveled across China to transmit the teachings of the Buddha. Thus, many ordinary Chinese may have had their own ideas and beliefs about foreigners, beliefs that are not necessarily represented in the sources mentioned and cited in this chapter. But Chinese records of the distant regions and peoples discussed here are vital sources not only for the study of China's interactions with the outside world but also for examining the history of many foreign regions, some of which did not leave any textual histories for posterity.

2

THE RISE OF CIVILIZATION IN
THE CENTRAL PLAINS

The remains of various subspecies of *Homo erectus* found in Yuanmou County in Yunnan Province, in Lantian County in Shaanxi Province, and at Zhoukoudian near Beijing suggest the existence of migratory trails from Africa to East Asia more than half a million years ago. Known as Yuanmou Man (*Homo erectus yuanmouensis*), Lantian Man (*Homo erectus lantianensis*), and Peking Man (*Homo erectus pekinensis*) respectively, these hominids produced distinctive stone tools. Some may have been able to control and use fire. Whether these hominids were ancestors of the modern Mongoloid Chinese is a controversial issue that remains unresolved, although an emerging consensus on the increasingly rich genetic data holds that there were multiple "out of Africa" events, including those for *Homo erectus* and *Homo sapiens*. Studies of the remains of *Homo erectus* and *Homo sapiens* in China make it clear that these species did not live in isolation. Moreover, there seem to have been "interactions and sustained migrations" between East Asian and European populations over a very long period of time (Keates 2004: 233).

The Neolithic cultures of China, such as the Yangshao (ca. 5000–3000 BCE) and Longshan (ca. 3000–2000 BCE), named after the sites where evidence of these cultures was first excavated, developed in the Yellow River valley. These Neolithic settlements extended from the modern province of Jiangsu in southern China to the northwestern provinces of Qinghai and Gansu. Archaeological evidence indicates extensive interactions not only among these settled societies but also with the nomadic tribes in the Central Asian steppe region. Foreign goods such as jade were most likely acquired by the Neolithic settlements located in present-day Qinghai and Gansu provinces, which bordered the Central Asian steppe region, and then passed on to the people in the Central Plains.

Human figurines found at several Neolithic sites are evidence of contacts with people outside the Central Plains. These figurines have Caucasoid

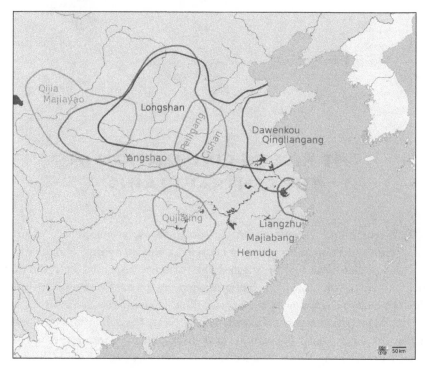

Map 2.1. Neolithic settlements in China.
(http://en.wikipedia.org/wiki/File:Neolithic_china.svg.)

features, large noses, deep eyes, and narrow faces (Liu 2004: 89–93) and may depict the agropastoral Indo-Europeans whose mummified bodies have been found in present-day Xinjiang Province.

The earliest of these so-called Tarim mummies dates from the beginning of the second millennium BCE (Mallory and Mair 2000). These people and their relatives on the steppe may have played an important role in introducing

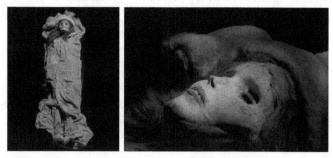

Figure 2.1. Mummy from Xinjiang (two views). (Photos by Wang Da-Gang.)

chariots and bronze-making technology to the Central Plains. The rest of this chapter examines these two technological imports as evidence of cross-cultural interaction between the Central Plains and foreign peoples in early Chinese history. It also describes the use of cowries, seashells that were utilized as currency, by the Shang dynasty as evidence of contacts between the Central Plains and the southern regions, extending to the Indian Ocean.[1]

THE ADVENT OF BRONZE METALLURGY

Bronze implements first emerged in Mesopotamia in the ancient Near East during the fourth millennium BCE. Made from alloyed copper and tin, bronze was harder than any previously known metal. Initially, bronze was used to manufacture weapons, but later agricultural implements, ritual vessels, and sculptures were also made from this new metal. In the Central Plains, evidence of bronze metallurgy first appears almost two millennia later, from sites belonging to the Erlitou Culture (ca. 2000–1500 BCE).[2] The bronze

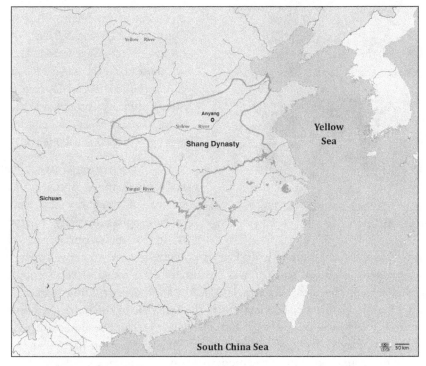

Map 2.2. The Shang dynasty.
(http://en.wikipedia.org/wiki/File:Shang_dynasty.svg.)

19

vessels found at the Erlitou sites date from circa 1700 to 1500 BCE. The technology needed to manufacture bronze seems to have been passed on to the Erlitou people by the neighboring Qijia and Siba cultures (among others), located in present-day Gansu Province, indicating an eastward transmission of bronze-making technology from Southwestern Eurasia through Central Asia to the Central Plains (Mei 2000).

That the use of bronze was widespread is evident from various archaeological sites belonging to the Shang dynasty. Exquisite bronze vessels, for example, have been discovered in large quantities at Anyang, one of the capitals of the Shang dynasty.

Figure 2.2. Shang bronze. (© Trustees of the British Museum.)

Many of these vessels are ritual items that were used either as containers for making offerings to dead ancestors or as burial items. In one of the royal tombs belonging to Lady Hao (Fu Hao), a consort of the Shang king Wu Ding (r. 1250–1192 BCE), 468 bronze objects were found. Many of these objects have delicate carvings and designs. During the Shang dynasty, bronze was also used to make weapons, chariots, and agricultural implements.

A fascinating aspect of Lady Hao's tomb is that it was so full of weaponry that some archaeologists initially mistook it for a male burial site. In truth, this martial aspect of Lady Hao is probably related to her northern or northwestern affinities, since it was customary for women of the steppe to fight alongside the men (Mallory 1991). Yet another intriguing instance of Lady Hao's long-distance connections is the fact that of the more than seven hundred jade pieces buried with her the majority have been shown, when chemically assayed, to be of eastern Central Asian origin (in particular from the region around Khotan in the modern region of Xinjiang).

Bronze-making technology also spread to other regional cultures in southwestern China, including cultures in the present-day provinces of Sichuan and Yunnan and even as far as what is now Thailand (White and Hamilton

Figure 2.3. Mask from Sanxingdui.
(www.cultural-china.com/chinaWH/html/en/
History246bye932.html.)

Figure 2.4. Statue from
Sanxingdui.
(www.cultural-china.com/
chinaWH/html/en/
History246bye933.html.)

2010). Bronze artifacts from the Sanxingdui site in Sichuan show close links between objects produced in the local region, but the ultimate origins of its metallurgical and cultural traditions are not clearly understood.

Two famous bronze artifacts from Sanxingdui are a large mask and a six-foot-tall statue. These artifacts indicate that the local craftsmen created their distinctive artistic tradition within an expanding Eurasian continental technology. Similarly, the bronze-making tradition of the Dian Culture (c. fourth century BCE to first century CE) in Yunnan possesses unique designs and molding techniques while displaying unmistakable affinities with steppe cultures to the north. One of the most striking bronze artifacts from the Dian Culture is a two-meter-long bronze coffin. There are also several bronze cowry containers, indicating, as discussed below, the trade and use of cowries in the Yunnan region.

The bronze pieces found at Shang, Sichuan, Yunnan, and other regional sites indicate that the metal was used mostly by the elite of these societies. Although weapons and agricultural tools were also made from bronze, the metal

Figure 2.5. Cowry container from Yunnan, Dian Culture. (Courtesy of Erich Lessing, Art Resource, New York.)

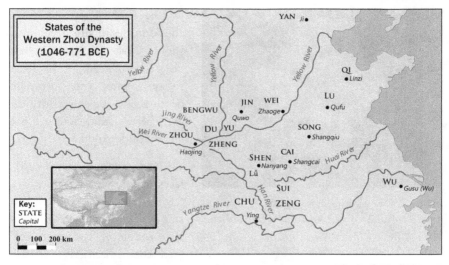

Map 2.3. The Western Zhou dynasty.
(http://en.wikipedia.org/wiki/File:EN-WesternZhouStates.jpg.)

was more frequently used for producing ritual items employed in ceremonies related to ancestor worship and funerary rites. The use of bronze to make ritual items continued during the Western Zhou period even after iron metallurgy was introduced to China, once again through Central Asia, in the first millennium BCE. In fact, it took about six centuries for iron eventually to replace bronze.

CHARIOTS AND HORSE RIDING

Chariots and horse-riding skills were similarly introduced to the Central Plains as a result of interactions between the settled peoples and nomadic tribes. While chariots were already in use during the Shang period and entered China as early as 1200 BCE (Shaughnessy 1988), horse-riding skills developed much later, perhaps as late as the fourth century BCE (Goodrich 1984). Archaeological remains and rock drawings clearly demonstrate an eastward transmission of chariotry from the Caucasus through Central Asia to China by 1600–1500 BCE.[3] A comparison of chariots used in China and those excavated in western Central Asia and the Near East shows striking similarities in regard to the number of spokes, location of axle, and wheel construction. Other resemblances suggest that the Chinese chariots used during the Shang and Zhou dynasties were derived from those used in the Caucasus, though with appropriate modifications for local conditions.

Initially, it seems, chariots were prestige items used mostly by Shang royalty in hunting expeditions rather than battles. There is some, albeit extremely limited, evidence of their use in battles during the Shang dynasty. This evidence, found in the form of inscriptions on Shang oracle bones, indicates that chariots were used by neighboring adversaries of the Shang to the north and northwest and sometimes captured from them. It was only during the Western Zhou period that the use of chariots became widespread in the Central Plains and they were employed as an important element of regional warfare. Still, even during this period chariots did not emerge as key strike weapons in battles in and around China but retained their chief role as mobile command and observation platforms. The use of chariots in warfare started to decline sometime in the fifth century BCE with the introduction of cavalry, another technological import from the Central Asian steppe.

Figure 2.6. Rock drawings of chariots. (After Shaughnessy 1988.)

Chariots ultimately proved difficult to maneuver in rough terrain, especially in hilly regions and land intersected by rivers, marshes, and other watery features. Domesticated horses were in use across most of Eurasia in the third millennium BCE, including by the pastoral nomadic tribes in the Central Asian steppe regions. While horses were used for chariots in Shang China, horse riding became prevalent only during the second half of the first millennium BCE. The reason for the late development of horse riding in China may have been cultural. The attire of the people in China, for example, was not convenient for riding horses. Proper gear, including trousers, belts, and saddles, was needed to foster the horse-riding tradition. Interactions with the Central Asian steppe people facilitated the introduction of such equestrian gear into China, and by the fourth century BCE cavalry and mounted archers had become integral parts of warfare among the warring states in the Yellow River valley. The use of cavalry created a demand for horses in China, which had limited pastoral lands in which to breed horses appropriate for warfare. Throughout most of its history, China had to depend on horses supplied by Central Asian and Tibetan traders. In fact, horses became one of the most important imports of the Chinese dynasties.

Commodities exchanged for horses included silk and tea, the latter especially during the Song and Ming periods, and princesses were occasionally married off to steppe rulers in order to secure horses or peace. When China was militarily strong, expeditions were sometimes launched to obtain horses by force.

Figure 2.7. Belt hooks. (© Trustees of the British Museum.)

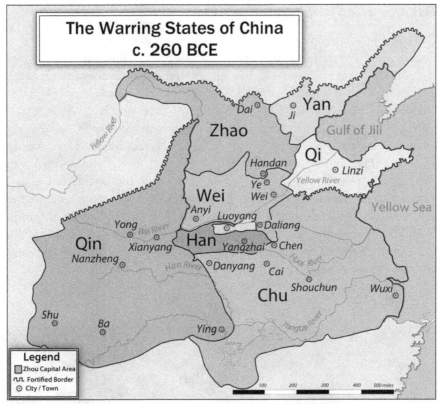

The Warring States of China
c. 260 BCE

Map 2.4. The Warring States period.
(http://en.wikipedia.org/wiki/File:EN-WarringStatesAll260BCE.jpg.)

Although rulers of China keenly recognized the power of the horse in the hands of nomadic warriors, a fundamental lack of affinity for this temperamental creature, which is difficult both to rear and to handle, meant that other means of projecting military strength had to be discovered. This the leaders of China found in the technique of massed infantry. The latter development resulted from the emergence of new modes of sociopolitical organization of human resources during the Warring States period (468–221 BCE) such as the extension of military service from the aristocracy to the peasantry; increasing complexity of the bureaucratic administration, including the creation of districts linked to the central government; and the emergence of a class of civil servants. Another key factor in the emergence of large, well-coordinated armies of foot soldiers was the widespread adoption of iron weapons. Supplying hundreds of thousands of soldiers with metal weapons had been unthinkable in the preceding Bronze Age, when bronze armaments were reserved exclusively for aristocratic members of society (Mair 2007).

THE CONNECTION TO THE SEAS

While early human migrations and the introduction of bronze metallurgy, chariots, and horse-riding traditions into the Central Plains demonstrate sustained contacts with Eurasia through land routes, evidence of the region's interaction with the maritime world comes from the presence of cowries in the Yellow River valley as early as the Neolithic period. Initially, it seems, cowries were used as jewelry and ritual items and eventually, during the Zhou dynasty, especially because they could not be counterfeited, as currency (Li 2006). Like bronze objects, cowries are found in Sichuan and Yunnan provinces. In fact, Yunnan may have been one of the thoroughfares through which cowries reached the Yellow River valley. A major source of cowries in China was the Maldives, a group of islands in the Indian Ocean, from which they were brought to the coastal regions of eastern India or Myanmar and then transported overland to Yunnan. Archaeological evidence indicates that cowries were in use in Yunnan at least from the second century BCE to the mid-seventeenth century CE (Pirazzoli-t'Serstevens 1990; Vogel 1993a, 1993b).

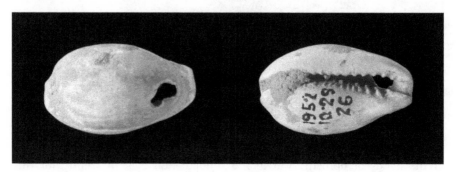

Figure 2.8. Cowries. (© Trustees of the British Museum.)

The Ryukyu Islands in the East China Sea may have been another source for cowries found in the Central Plains. These cowries most likely were transported along the eastern coast of China and up the Yellow River to the Central Plains. Although there is no evidence that people from Central Plains were active in maritime activities at this early stage, the region clearly had access to commodities traded in the maritime world. Scholars have suggested the existence of a so-called Nusantao trading and communication network of the Southeast Asian natives that, since at least the third millennium BCE, linked the maritime world from the Pacific to the Indian Ocean and especially the coastal regions of China to Japan, Korea, and Southeast Asia (Solheim 2000). Thus, it appears that China, rather than developing in isolation as had long been commonly believed, actually maintained prolonged contacts with the outside world through both overland and maritime routes.

THE NAME CHINA AND CONTACT WITH THE WIDER WORLD

Interactions between China and the neighboring regions intensified after 771 BCE, when the Zhou dynasty gradually started disintegrating and the regional governors began asserting more autonomy. In order to expand their territories, these regional governors began encroaching on the areas settled or used as pastoral lands by their tribal neighbors. These conflicts between the expanding states of the Central Plains and peoples in the border areas may have been the reason for the unfalteringly antagonistic and exoticized portrayals of foreign people that show up in the later historical records in China. These records also indicate that, in addition to armed conflicts, economic exchanges between China and the neighboring societies intensified. Indeed, various commodities from China, including silk, became lucrative items of trade to members of the neighboring societies both for internal consumption and for reexport to other regions.

The Qin state (897–206 BCE), which was located on the western periphery of China and eventually unified the region in 221 BCE, appears to have played an important role in supplying goods from China to the nomadic tribes in Central Asia. It is perhaps for this reason that some of these commodities acquired the prefix *cina-* (literally "of China") and appear in foreign records, especially those in India. Hides (*cinasi*), vermilion (*cinapista*), peaches (*cinani*), pears (*cinarajaputra*), camphor (*cinka*), and silk (*cinamsuka*) all appear in Indian sources as products of "China." In the aggregate, they appear to be the first records to bear the modern name China, most likely derived from the name of the Qin state.

Thus, it is clear from archæological and textual sources that extensive cross-cultural networks, comprising the movement of people, goods, and ideas, connected the Central Plains to the wider world long before the famed Silk Road was established. To the north and northwest, China maintained contacts with nomadic tribes that contributed to the transfer of bronze and iron metallurgies. These tribes also passed on horse-riding skills and the technology required for manufacturing chariots to the people in the Central Plains. To the south, the people living in the Yellow River valley seem to have had sustained interactions with the settled societies in Sichuan and Yunnan. And through some of these regions, the Central Plains were connected to the wider maritime world.

3

THE FORMATION AND DEVELOPMENT
OF THE SILK ROUTES

B y the time the Qin state unified China in 221 BCE, significant developments had taken place elsewhere in the world. In 558 BCE, Cyrus (r. 558–530 BCE) established the Persian Achaemenid empire (558–330 BCE) in modern-day Iran, which, under the succeeding rulers Cambyses (r. 530–522 BCE) and Darius (r. 521–486 BCE), extended its rule from the Indus Valley region in southern Asia to Anatolia (present-day Turkey) and into Egypt. About two centuries later, invasion by the Macedonian ruler Alexander (r. 336–323 BCE) resulted in the collapse of the Achaemenids and the founding of Greek colonies in Asia (the Seleucid) and Egypt (the Ptolemaic). Alexander's conquest of the Achaemenids and his plans to march into regions beyond the Indus Valley also brought about changes in southern Asia. The impending attack led to internal problems, eventual disintegration, and ultimately the collapse of the kingdom of Magadha, which was located in the central Ganges River valley region. The person responsible for overthrowing the kingdom of Magadha was Chandragupta Maurya (r. ca. 320–ca. 298 BCE), who, with the help of his skillful adviser Kautilya, established the Mauryan empire (ca. 320–ca. 185 BCE) in southern Asia. In Italy, the Romans created a republican constitution in 509 BCE and, despite internal problems, conquered various regions of western Europe and parts of northern Africa.

These developments contributed to the formation of long-distance trade routes that stimulated cross-continental interactions and exchanges. Indeed, the political stability throughout vast regions of Asia and Europe brought about by these empires was conducive to the movement of people and goods not only within the specific regions but also across the continents. Commercial exchange was also stimulated by policies that standardized weights and measures, built and protected highways, and encouraged internal and external commerce. Consequently, commercial activity along some of the routes between China and foreign regions discussed in the previous chapter intensified and eventually integrated the Yellow River valley into the expanding network of cross-continental interactions. The routes that connected China to the markets in the west are popularly known as the Silk Roads (*Die Seidenstrassen*), a name given to the route that passed through Central Asia by the German geographer Ferdinand von Richthofen in 1877.

CENTRAL ASIA AND CHINA

The Central Asian region was the primary link between China and the empires mentioned above. As discussed in chapter 2, contacts between China and Central Asia dated back to the second millennium BCE. The formation of empires in Persia, South Asia, and Europe significantly augmented the role of the Central Asian region in China's contacts with the outside world. However, Central Asia was also a cause for concern and a target for the expanding empires located in China.

Although the Qin dynasty lasted less than two decades and was despised by later court historians for the brutal persecution of its subjects, especially intellectuals, it was instrumental in integrating China into a single, bureaucratically organized state. It standardized the Chinese script, currencies, weights, axle widths, and laws. It also built new roads, bridges, and irrigation systems that were conducive to the expansion of commerce and agriculture. The Qin dynasty is also credited with connecting the defensive walls of the previous kingdoms into what became known as the Great Wall. The connection and construction of new sections of the wall were related to the Qin state's ongoing conflicts with the nomadic people of Central Asia known as the Xiongnu, an adversary of the Chinese empire and trading partner of other regional powers in Central Asia.[1] It was through interactions with nomadic tribes such as the Xiongnu that horseback riding and mounted archery had been introduced into China during the waning years of the Warring States period. Military confrontations between the states in East Asia and the Xiongnu were common, and some sections of the Great Wall were built as a consequence of this warfare.

Shortly after its unification of China, the Qin dynasty, in 214 BCE, successfully invaded Xiongnu territories in the Ordos region. Conflict with the Xiongnu emerged as one of the main concerns of the Han dynasty, which succeeded the Qin in 206 BCE and ruled China for about four hundred years (divided almost exactly in half into the Western Han, also known as the Former Han, and the Eastern Han, also known as the Later Han). By the time the Han dynasty was established, wars and economic interactions with the states in China had transformed the Xiongnu from groups of nomadic tribes into a powerful unified confederacy. When it became clear to the early rulers of the Han dynasty that military confrontation with the powerful Xiongnu would prove futile, they devised a diplomatic policy of appeasement called *heqin* (peace and alliance). Under this policy, the Han court sought to establish peaceful relationships with the Xiongnu in exchange for various economic and other incentives. It initiated, for example, a marriage alliance with the Xiongnu leader by giving him a Han princess. The Han court also recognized the Xiongnu as an equal brother state and sent annual gifts that included silk, gold, and rice wine (Yü 1967). A treaty between the Han court and the Xiongnu outlining these provisions was signed in 198 BCE.

The ascendancy of the Xiongnu also had a significant impact on the other nomadic tribes that occupied eastern Central Asia. The Yuezhi, an Indo-European group, was one of those most affected by the expansion of Xiongnu power. After resisting several Xiongnu incursions, the Yuezhi were thoroughly defeated in 162 BCE and, according to a famous legend, the skull of their king was made into a drinking cup by the Xiongnu ruler. After this defeat, the Yuezhi were forced to flee westward, ultimately to the region beyond the Pamirs.[2]

Twenty years later, when the Han court began rethinking its policy toward the Xiongnu, Emperor Wu decided to contact the Yuezhi to propose a military alliance against their common adversary. The diplomat sent to Central Asia to accomplish this task, Zhang Qian (d. 114 BCE), left the Han capital sometime in 139 BCE but was soon captured by the Xiongnu. He was forced to marry a local woman and remained a captive for about ten years. Zhang managed to escape and eventually made contact with the Yuezhi. He discovered, however, that the Yuezhi—having found a new life in Central Asia—were not interested in fighting the Xiongnu.

Even though the Han court failed to find an ally, it launched a surprise attack on the Xiongnu in 129 BCE. During the next decade, the Xiongnu and the Han armies fought two major battles, in 121 and 119, in which the latter emerged as clear victors. These defeats led to the breakup of the Xiongnu empire and the entry of Han forces into the Central Asian region, reaching as far west as Samarkand.

After occupying Central Asia, the Han court quickly set up protectorates and military garrisons to control and administer the region. It also established agricultural garrisons to provide supplies to the Han forces stationed in Central Asia. Additionally, the court attempted to interfere in the political affairs of the Indo-Greek kingdoms located near its western borders, which Alexander had established earlier. The Jibin kingdom (Kapisa-Gandhara) in

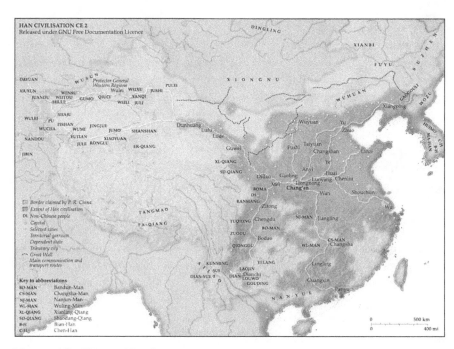

Map 3.1. The Western Han dynasty.
(http://en.wikipedia.org/wiki/File:Han_Civilisation.png.)

the southern Hindu Kush region seems to have been one of the main targets of the Han court. Accusing the Jibin rulers of assaulting the Han envoys frequenting the region, the court allied itself with a local Greek settler in an attempt to change the regime in the Hindu Kush kingdom. Although it succeeded in placing him on the throne, the relationship between the court and the new ruler, known in Chinese sources as Yinmofu (Hermaeus?), turned bitter, with the result that hostilities between the Han and Jibin continued until the end of the first millennium BCE. The antagonism between the Han court and the Jibin kingdom may have stemmed from the fact that the local rulers in the Hindu Kush region were adamantly opposed to Han expansionist policies in Central Asia (Sen 2003: 3–4; Yu 1998). These exchanges are important illustrations of the role and participation of the Chinese in Eurasian intercultural interactions before the Common Era.

The Han dominated the eastern Central Asian region for about a century, when internal problems associated with land reforms weakened the dynasty. A usurper called Wang Mang (r. 9–23 CE) overthrew the Han and briefly established a new dynasty known as Xin (9–23). Within two decades, however, one of the descendants of the Han ruling family reclaimed the Mandate of Heaven and quickly reasserted its dominance over Central Asia. Under the occupation by this "Later Han" dynasty, the oasis towns around the Taklamakan Desert witnessed rapid growth, especially with the expansion of agricultural garrisons and the influx of immigrants from the Yellow River valley.[3] Gradually these settlements developed into key towns on the Silk Routes.

THE FORMATION OF THE SILK ROADS

Regular exchange of goods between the settled societies around the Yellow River valley and the nomadic peoples in Inner and Central Asia seems to have begun as early as the second millennium BCE. By the latter half of the first millennium BCE, when cavalry units were formed within the armies of states in China, economic relationships with Central Asian peoples became particularly vital for the supply of horses. Since China did not produce horses that fit the needs of cavalries, the Central Asian steppe region was its main source for this important commodity. Indeed, as noted above, horses remained one of the leading imports of later Chinese dynasties.

One of the ways in which the Han and subsequent dynasties acquired horses from Central Asia was through the tributary system. As discussed in chapter 2, the Chinese dynasties believed that their emperors were the Sons of Heaven, who had to be recognized as such by all the neighboring peoples. To show that they "submitted" to the Chinese emperor and recognized him as the ruler of All under Heaven (*tianxia*), these peoples were expected to regularly send tributary missions to the Chinese courts. The missions carried native and foreign commodities, and they were often rewarded with cash or Chinese goods in return for their "submission." While the system satisfied the political and ethnic notions of superiority of the Chinese ruler, it was also an economic arrangement that appeared to benefit both sides. The Chinese court acquired the goods it desired, and tribute bearers' trips to the court offered them an opportunity to trade, albeit illegally, at local markets. Chinese court officials were often concerned about the true intentions of the tribute carriers. In the first century BCE, for instance, a Han official named Du Qin complained that most of the tribute bearers from the Jibin kingdom were profit-seeking traders and not high-ranking officials or nobles. Despite such concerns, imperial officials were aware of the economic function of the tributary system. In fact, in order to reach a peaceful settlement with the Xiongnu, the Han court used what was clearly a reverse form of the tributary system.

Horses of diverse qualities were presented to the Han ruler by envoys from various Central Asian kingdoms. The most desired horses at the Han court were those from Ferghana, described in Chinese sources as "blood-sweating horses" because of occasional bleeding from the skin caused by a parasite. The

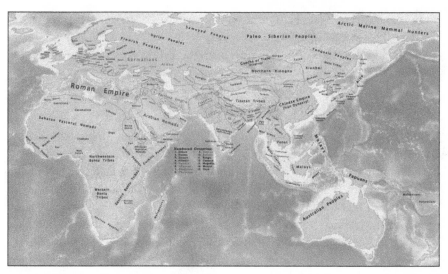

Map 3.2. The world in 50 CE.
(Map by Thomas Lessman. www.WorldHistoryMaps.info.)

Han court often offered silk fabrics and floss as return gifts. At the frontier markets, official and unofficial trading of horses and silk was common. For the Central Asian kingdoms and nomads, the possession of silk conveyed prestige and an opportunity to trade in markets farther west, where this valuable commodity was transported to southern Asia and the Mediterranean.

It was perhaps not until the end of the first century BCE that the routes known as the "Silk Roads" started taking shape. By this time, not only had the Han empire occupied parts of Central Asia and triggered the development of the oasis towns skirting the Taklamakan Desert, but the Romans had also extended their rule over the eastern Mediterranean and occupied Egypt. The establishment by a branch of the Yuezhi of the Kushana empire (ca. first to fourth century CE), which stretched from present-day Afghanistan to eastern India, contributed to the strengthening of commercial and cultural links between China and other areas of Asia and Europe. Roman and Yuezhi traders were among the most active along the routes that connected these regions. Many of them traded in silk from China, which was carried, usually on camels, through Central Asia to ports in southern Asia and from there to Roman provinces on the Red and Mediterranean seas. Lapis lazuli from Afghanistan, Roman glassware, South Asian spices, and other commodities such as amber, gems, and fragrances became mainstays of this trade.

China was connected to the markets in the Mediterranean through both an overland and a maritime route. The overland route linked the Han cities of Chang'an and Luoyang to the oasis towns of Turfan and Khotan on the northern and southern rims of the Taklamakan Desert. From these Taklamakan towns goods originating in China were transported either to Persia or to Barbaricon and Barygaza, two coastal towns in southern Asia. While land routes connected Persia to the Mediterranean markets, sea routes across the Arabian Sea from Barbaricon and Barygaza linked southern Asia to Egypt through the Red Sea. Goods from the Mediterranean Sea reached China through the same overland routes.

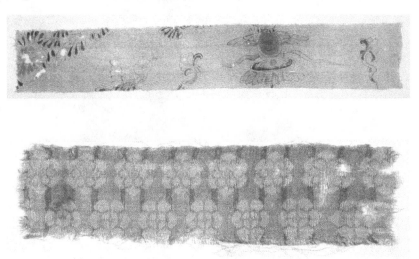

Figure 3.1. Silk textiles. (© Trustees of the British Museum.)

The early first century CE also witnessed the development of a maritime route from the Mediterranean to China. This route was divided into three important sectors: the first from the Red Sea to the coastal regions of the Indian subcontinent, the second from the Indian coasts to Southeast Asia, and the third from Southeast Asia to Guangzhou (Canton). Initially, ships traveled close to the coastline, but with the development of shipbuilding, advances in navigational technology, and enhanced knowledge of monsoon winds, maritime trade became better organized, faster, more profitable, and sometimes safer than overland trade. The Romans, for example, found the maritime route more convenient for trading with southern Asia because the Parthians in Iran often tried to control the overland commerce passing through their territories. Roman traders used the maritime route to procure goods from China and the Indian subcontinent, through Barygaza and Barbaricon, and from ports such as Muziris and Poduca in southern India (Liu and Shaffer 2007: 46–52).

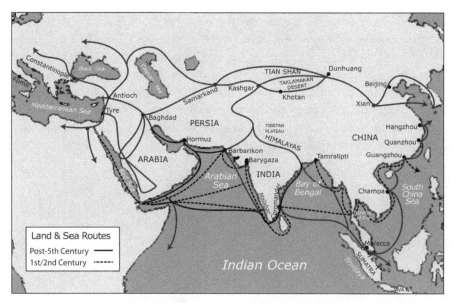

Map 3.3. The Silk Routes.

Traders from the Kushan kingdom, southern India, and Southeast Asia engaged in commerce across the latter two sectors of the maritime route. Their maritime networks extended from the Indian subcontinent to southern Vietnam and present-day Guangzhou (in Guangdong Province) and Hepu (in Guangxi Province), regions that were occupied by the Han dynasty in the late second century BCE. Glassware from Rome and other luxury goods, such as kingfisher feathers, rhinoceros horns, and precious stones, may have been sold at these coastal ports even before their occupation by the Han. The Han court is known to have created bureaucratic mechanisms to oversee the maritime trade and tributary missions arriving by sea. This attracted more foreign merchants to the seaports, some of whom settled down at these sites, establishing diasporas that continued to stimulate maritime exchanges with Indian Ocean states for many centuries.

According to Zhang Qian, there may have been another route through which commodities from China were exported to southern and Central Asia. After returning to the Han court, having failed to persuade the Yuezhi to form an alliance with the Han dynasty to fight the Xiongnu, Zhang Qian reported to the emperor that there might be another route to Central Asia that did not pass through the Xiongnu territories. Zhang Qian noted that when he was in Bactria—located in present day Afghanistan—he saw bamboo and cloth made in what is now the Sichuan region in local markets there.[4] He was told that these commodities reached Bactria through "Shendu," a

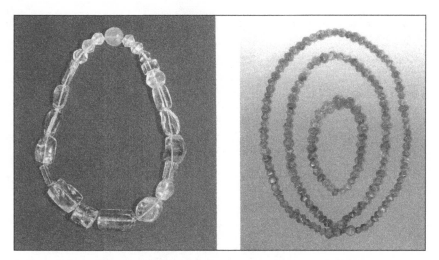

Figure 3.2. Glass beads. (After Wu 2006.)

region that included northern parts of the Indian subcontinent. Based on this information, Zhang Qian concluded that there must be a route that linked the southwestern regions of China to Bactria through the Indian subcontinent. He convinced the Han emperor to search for this route. But after a number of attempts, the Han court failed to find this route because of resistance from local tribes in present-day Yunnan Province.

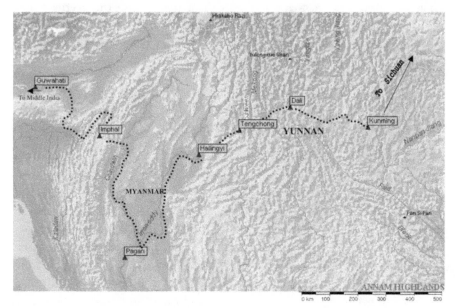

Map 3.4. The Yunnan-India route. (After Sen 2003.)

We must remember that the lands south of the Yangtze were originally populated by indigenous peoples, and the farther south one went the less control was exercised by the northern Chinese courts. Despite repeated attempts to "pacify" these malaria-infested regions, large tracts remained beyond the reach of Chinese authority throughout most of history.

The route to which Zhang Qian referred may have been the one through which cowries from the Maldives were brought to the Yellow River valley during the Shang dynasty (see chapter 2). Unlike the other two routes noted above, trading activity on this path seems to have been undertaken by local groups and tribes rather than established trading groups. It was only after the seventh century that trading and other cultural exchanges through this southwestern route grew rapidly. The route was subsequently integrated with other major overland and maritime routes. But, while it is also termed a "Silk Road," the "Southwestern Silk Road" to be specific, there is little evidence that silk was one of the main commodities traded along this route.

Together, these three routes (the Central Asian, maritime, and the Southwestern) connected China to various parts of the world. These routes were not only conduits for trade and the exchange of goods; they were also passages through which the exchange of peoples, technologies, and ideas took place. Chapter 2 outlined the overland transmission of bronze making and horseback riding from Central Asia to China. With the expansion of the Han dynasty into Central Asia and the growth of trade along the overland and maritime routes, Sogdian and Indo-Scythian merchants started venturing into the urban centers and port cities of China. Some of them were instrumental in introducing foreign cultural ideas and traditions into China. The most important of such traditions was undoubtedly Buddhism, which originated in southern Asia.

THE TRANSMISSION OF BUDDHISM

A number of philosophical traditions had developed in China before Buddhist teachings penetrated Chinese society. By the Neolithic period, the idea of ancestor worship already seems to have been established among the people living in China. The use of bronze ritual vessels and the practice of cracking oracle bones during the Shang dynasty indicate that the veneration of ancestors was widespread during the second millennium BCE. Deceased ancestors, according to the beliefs of the Shang people, influenced and even dictated the lives of the living. Various rituals and ceremonies were performed to satisfy the postmortem needs of the dead. The offering of food and liquor at the tombs of ancestors was a common method of venerating them. In the sixth century

Figure 3.3. Oracle bone. (http://www2.hawaii.edu/~kjolly/151/04shangorac.htm.)

BCE, Kongzi (Confucius, 551–479 BCE) incorporated this ancient tradition into one of his core teachings. He emphasized that filial children must not only look after their parents when they are alive but also venerate them after their deaths. This esteem for filial piety still shapes the social relationships and belief systems of the peoples of China and neighboring regions.

Confucian teachings, formulated by Confucius and later developed by Mengzi (Mencius, 372–289 BCE) and Xunzi (ca. 312–230 BCE), underscored the importance of education and an understanding of the past to foster the virtues of filial piety, loyalty, obedience, brotherliness, and friendship in the creation of "superior individuals." These benevolent, kindhearted, superior persons, endowed with etiquette and knowledge of proper rituals and ceremonies, were expected to contribute to the establishment of a peaceful and stable society that was devoid of selfish interests. These teachings, however, failed to have the impact on contemporary politics that Confucius aspired to bring about until the Han dynasty, several centuries after his death. At the Han court, especially during the reign of Emperor Wu, Confucianism and Confucian scholars started gaining official support. Some of these scholars were appointed to official posts, beginning the dominance of Confucianism in court affairs. In fact, during later periods a Confucian education became the primary means through which commoners could enter the government bureaucracy.

At the folk level another tradition, which later developed as religious Daoism, was taking root. Perhaps the first clear manifestation of this movement began in the guise of what is known as Huang-Lao proto-Daoism, which flourished in the second century BCE. The name Huang-Lao is most likely a contraction of Huangdi (the Yellow Emperor, a mythical founding ruler) and Laozi (the "Old Master"), who in the second century CE would be deified as the embodiment of the transcendent Way (Tao/Dao).

During the same period, around the middle of the second century and thereafter, several other significant developments in the history of Chinese popular religion took place. Chief among these were Great Peace Daoism (Taiping Dao), Heavenly Masters Daoism (Tianshi Dao), and the Yellow Turban Rebellion (in 184 CE). The first, which emerged in the east, was an attempt to create a paradise on earth, with great attention paid to administrative units and bureaucratic control, constituting a veritable theocratic state. The second, also known as Five Pecks of Rice Daoism (named for the tax that had to be paid to the authorities), proliferated in the west (especially Sichuan) and ultimately led to the establishment of an elaborate politico-religious organization, elements of which have lasted to the present day. The third, which grew out of the first, had more overt political and military ambitions, the aim of its leaders being nothing less than the overthrow of the Han dynasty. Although they did not realize their millenarian goal, the weakened government never recovered, and it collapsed in 220 CE.

Elsewhere in the world, the sixth and fifth centuries BCE witnessed the emergence of important philosophical and religious traditions. Socrates (470–399 BCE) in Athens, somewhat like Confucius, taught that ethical and moral values were imperative to the establishment of a just society. In Persia, under the Achaemenid empire, Zoroastrian ideas of duality and the importance of human morality within the context of a cosmic battle between good and evil were becoming influential.[5] But the development most relevant to the history of China was the emergence of Buddhism in South Asia. Gautama Siddhartha (ca. fifth century BCE), a contemporary of Confucius, formulated his teachings about the way to end suffering caused by desire and craving. His teachings had a profound impact on almost every society in Asia.

The Buddha (Awakened One), as Siddhartha was known after he attained *bodhi* (awakening to the truth about suffering and its cessation), believed that the continuous cycle of birth, death, and rebirth (*samsara*) entails endless suffering caused by desire. To end this suffering, one had to detach oneself from desires and cravings and follow an eightfold path, including practicing such behaviors as right views, right speech, and right concentration, to reach the stage of nirvana (cessation of the cycle of birth, death, and rebirth). A key step toward detachment from desire and craving was the renunciation of social

Figure 3.4. The Buddha. (© Trustees of the British Museum.)

life in order to become a member of the monastic community known as the *sangha*. Meditative practices (*dhyana*) and the pursuit of strict monastic rules (*vinaya*) were essential if the adept was to maintain detachment from society and concentrate on attaining enlightenment and nirvana.

By the first century BCE, additional beliefs had been introduced into Buddhist teachings, which attracted new followers to the religion. These new teachings included the concept of bodhisattvas (enlightened beings), who delayed reaching nirvana themselves to help others understand and follow the teachings of the Buddha. Also new to Buddhist teachings was the veneration of Buddhist figures as divinities. Both developments became important aspects of the set of Buddhist traditions known as Mahayana (Greater Vehicle).

Apparently, these later teachings of Buddhism entered China in the first century CE, when one of the cousins of the Han ruler Ming (r. 28–75) is reported to have provided vegetarian feasts to Buddhist monks and laypersons. But neither archaeological nor textual evidence provides clear proof of the existence of Buddhist institutions in China at this early stage. It is only in the second century that archaeological evidence for the presence of Buddhism in the Han empire begins to emerge. One of the earliest items of evidence comes from the coastal city of Lianyungang in the present-day province of Jiangsu in northeastern China. Engraved on the boulders of Mount Kongwang near Lianyungang are images of the Buddha in standing, seated, and parinirvana (lying in perfect quietude) postures; representations of the *jataka* tales (stories of the Buddha's prior rebirths); foreign donor figures; secular figures (perhaps traders) wearing foreign dress usually identified as of Kushana style; and the

Figure 3.5. The Buddha in the parinirvana posture, Mount Kongwang, Jiangsu Province. (After Sen 2003.)

traditional Chinese motif of a moon and a toad together with the Queen Mother of the West. These images date from the late second century and suggest the presence of a foreign diasporic community, either Indo-Scythian or Parthian, in the region. These foreigners seem to have been influenced by Buddhist, as well as local, Chinese beliefs. Indeed, the Mount Kongwang images indicate the early amalgamation of Buddhist teachings and Chinese ideas.

The mixing of Buddhist ideas with native Chinese beliefs can also be discerned in Han period tombs excavated in Sichuan and Gansu provinces and the southwestern reaches of the Yangzi River. At Mahao in Sichuan Province, for example, small images of the Buddha were carved on the rear lintel of a tomb that dates to the late second or early third century. Additionally, the structure of the tomb resembles Buddhist caves found in western Central Asia. The use of Buddhist images in Han tombs suggests that the Chinese perceived the Buddha as an immortal being, a good omen in funerary decoration capable of granting immortality to dead souls (Wu 1986). In fact, it is evident that the Chinese were initially drawn to the mortuary implications of Buddhism.

Their understanding of the religion at this initial stage was limited and could have derived only from contact with foreign traders and devotional representations. The arrival of Buddhist monks, and the translation and proselytizing activities they undertook, changed this to some extent. But, for the greater part of the history of the Buddhist doctrine in China, the practice of Buddhism among common Chinese remained a mixture of the teachings of the Buddha and their own local and folk beliefs.

Figure 3.6. Image of the Buddha in a Han dynasty tomb. (After *Wenwu* 5 [1980].)

Two important points need to be made regarding the early transmission of Buddhism to the Han empire. First, the images of Buddhism in Han China predate the establishment of Buddhist institutions in eastern Central Asia and Southeast Asia. This would suggest that Buddhist ideas were initially transmitted over a long distance rather than directly introduced from either Central or Southeast Asia. Also important to note is that the early translators and proselytizers of Buddhism were not from southern Asia but from Iran and Sogdiana, located in part of present-day Uzbekistan. These two points are significant for understanding the complex Buddhist networks—discussed in the next chapter—that connected most of the societies in Asia.

4

CHINA AND THE BUDDHIST WORLD

The traders and urban centers that connected China to southern Asia were crucial for the successful transmission of Buddhist doctrines. As mentioned in chapter 3, traders, rather than religious missionaries, were likely to have introduced Buddhist ideas into the Han empire. Urban centers, on the other hand, provided supporting mechanisms, such as markets, resting places, and rich donors, to long-distance traders and monastic communities. In fact, the spread of Buddhism within southern Asia was also facilitated by long-distance trading activity and urban growth. Both textual and archaeological evidence indicates that a majority of the early Buddhist monastic institutions in southern Asia emerged near towns with support from the merchant class. The same seems to be true for the transmission of Buddhist doctrines and practices from southern Asia to China. By linking the towns and ports of southern Asia to those in the Han empire through intermediary regions of Central and Southeast Asia, long-distance traders helped to stimulate the exchange of Buddhist ideas and paraphernalia. During later periods, trading routes were also crucial for the spread of Buddhist doctrines from China to neighboring kingdoms in Korea and Japan. This intimate association among mercantile activity, urban centers, and the transmission of Buddhist doctrines created complex networks of cross-cultural exchange that integrated China with the rest of Asia. These networks featured the exchange of secular and religious goods, transmission of cultural ideas and scientific technologies, pilgrimage activity, and diplomatic interactions.

BUDDHISM IN CHINA

The transmission of Buddhism to Han China presented a conundrum to both the transmitters of the religion and the people who wanted to follow the new faith. While in the initial phase the misperception of the Buddha as a Daoist-style longevity-granting deity contributed to its spread eastward, for the religion to take root in a new society it was important to introduce its characteristic worldviews and teachings which were different and sometimes contradictory to beliefs that originated in China. There were major linguistic differences, a distinct array of allegories, and a set of social values and eschatological views that contrasted with those shaped by Confucian ideas of filial piety. In addition, those who wanted to maintain the traditional beliefs were always quick to point out the foreign (and thus "barbarian") origins of Buddhism.

To address these issues, the transmitters of Buddhism used a wide range of techniques and methods to make the Buddhist doctrine more easily accessible to Chinese followers and, at the same time, to present it as a legitimate religion. This was achieved at the cost of transforming the religion in various ways so that it became more Chinese than Indian. This process of transformation is usually called the "Sinification of Buddhism." During this process, China itself emerged as a central realm of Buddhism, where monks from other Asian societies came to learn the doctrine and pay homage to various Buddhist divinities.

The painstaking process of translating the teachings of the Buddha into Chinese was a key reason for the successful transmission of Buddhism. Sometimes these translations were made from texts brought to China by foreign missionaries and Chinese pilgrims who had visited southern Asia. At other times, the teachings were rendered into Chinese-language texts through oral transmission. Since there were exceedingly few bilingual specialists, the arduous task of translation was often undertaken collaboratively: one person read or orally narrated the teachings in the original Indian language, a second person translated them into Chinese, a third person wrote down the Chinese translation, and a fourth edited and proofread the translated text. In addition to the difficulty of accurately translating Indian languages, these translators also faced the complex task of introducing Indian concepts to Chinese audiences. As a result, some of the early Buddhist texts rendered into Chinese were selections of elementary teachings of Buddhism on suffering, retribution, and continuous birth rather than complicated philosophical treatises. These teachings were usually employed to proselytize to the common people through roadside storytelling and pictorial representations often framed within folk ideas and local beliefs.

The rendering of Indian languages and ideas had a widespread impact on Chinese society. While the translations were instrumental in introducing new vocabulary and literary genres, the amalgamation of Buddhist ideas of rebirth with Daoist views on human longevity captured the imagination of the Chinese people concerning the pains of postmortem punishments as well

Figure 4.1. The Chinese Buddhist hell. (© Trustees of the British Museum.)

as the joys of paradise. Indeed, by the sixth century, the Chinese view of the afterlife was completely transformed because of the introduction of Buddhist ideas and teachings.

A second reason for the initial success of Buddhism in China was the chaotic political situation that followed the collapse of the Han dynasty in 220 CE. The unstable situation raised questions about the validity of Confucian-organized statecraft and resulted in the increasing popularity of other religious teachings, especially those advocated by the followers of Daoism. Some Buddhist ideas, mixed with local beliefs, also became attractive to those seeking alternative ways to achieve religious salvation. This was especially true of the fused Buddho-Chinese messianic tradition, which anticipated the coming of a savior. This belief led to the popularity of the cult of the future Buddha known as Maitreya.

The support granted to Buddhism by some of the smaller states that succeeded the Han was a third factor that contributed to the establishment of the South Asian religion as one of the three main belief systems of China. Examples of such states include the Northern Wei (386–534) and the Liang (502–57) dynasties. Founded by a northern people called the Tabgach (Tuoba), one of the successor groups of the Central Asian Xiongnu, the Northern Wei brought Buddhist institutions under state control and sponsored the construction of large-scale Buddhist monuments, including the magnificent cave temples at Yungang (near the city of Datong). During the reign of the Tuoba Wei, the city of Luoyang, once the capital of the Han dynasty, emerged as a major site for Buddhist practice and learning in East Asia. In 477, it had about one hundred Buddhist temples and two thousand monks and nuns (Ch'en 1964: 155). Here, too, the Northern Wei rulers sponsored

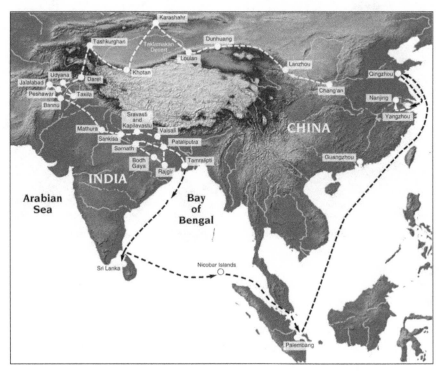

Map 4.1. Faxian's pilgrimage to India. (After Sen 2006.)

the construction of a grand series of caves filled with Buddhist sculptures carved out of stone at a site called Longmen. On the other hand, in the south Emperor Wu (502–49) of the Liang dynasty used Buddhism to legitimize his imperial power and support Buddhist establishments in the southern regions of China; he is known to have converted to Buddhism. Buddhist monks served as his advisers and, modeling himself on the Indian Buddhist king Ashoka, he forbade the use of animals in religious sacrifices.

In addition to the sponsorship of Buddhist temples and construction of religious monuments, these dynasties—both in the north and in the south—also sponsored translation activities at state monasteries. These court-sponsored translation projects usually involved a large number of monks and officials and elaborate rituals and ceremonies. The state support for Buddhism peaked under the Sui (589–618) emperor Yang, who reunified China in 589. Like Emperor Wu, he modeled himself on the Indian monarch Ashoka and used Buddhist rituals and ceremonies to unify his newly established empire under Buddhist ideology. One of these rituals was the distribution and enshrinement of the relics of the Buddha at various sites across his kingdom. These elaborate relic-enshrinement ceremonies usually lasted seven days and involved court and local officials. By the time of the Sui dynasty, China clearly had emerged as a leading Buddhist center outside southern Asia.

A final feature that led to Buddhism taking root in China was the continuous flow of monks and Buddhist artifacts from southern Asia. In 399, Faxian became the first Chinese monk to travel to the birthplace of the Buddha and return to write his travelog, *A Record of the Buddhist Kingdoms*. Faxian is supposed to have been around sixty when he embarked on the trip to southern Asia. Although he notes that the purpose of his trip was to procure the monastic rules (*vinaya*) for the proper functioning of Buddhist communities in China, it is clear that he also planned a pilgrimage to the sites and places related to the life of the Buddha. As a result, Faxian's records mostly deal with descriptions of sacred Buddhist sites and the activities of the historical Buddha and his supporters. Faxian's work seems to have had a tremendous impact not only on the Buddhist community in China but also among the non-Buddhist literati. Many of the descriptions of southern Asia in the fifth and sixth centuries are based on Faxian's records. And, as noted in chapter 1,

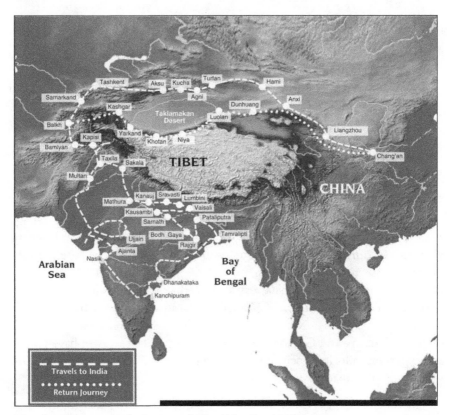

Map 4.2. Xuanzang's pilgrimage to India. (After Sen 2006.)

49

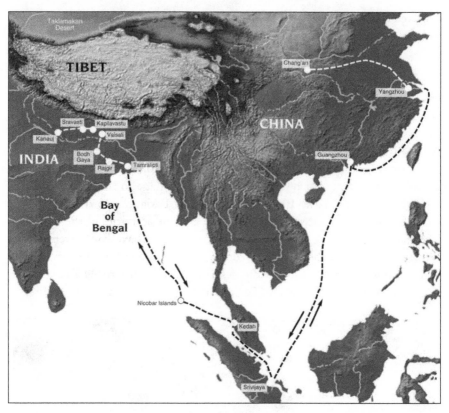

Map 4.3. Yijing's pilgrimage to India. (After Sen 2006.)

Faxian's account of the region was crucial in creating the perception of ancient India as a civilized and advanced society almost on a par with China.

Faxian's successful trip also inspired other Chinese monks to make pilgrimages to India. The two most renowned were Xuanzang and Yijing, both of whom visited southern Asia in the seventh century. In addition to visiting pilgrimage sites and procuring Buddhist texts, Xuanzang actively pursued close relationships with two of the most powerful contemporary rulers of southern Asia: Harsha, the king of the vast kingdom of Kanauj in northern India, and Kumara of Kamarupa, located in eastern India. On his return to Tang China, Xuanzang became the favorite religious teacher of emperors Taizong and Gaozong. At the Tang court, he seems to have played an important role in procuring state support for Buddhist activities and sponsoring diplomatic missions to southern Asia.

In the sixteenth century Xuanzang's journey to India was transformed into an immensely popular novel called *Xiyou ji* (Journey to the West), which was eventually made into an equally popular TV series by the People's Republic of China.

The monk Yijing's journey to southern Asia is also noteworthy for several reasons. Yijing, who embarked on his trip in 671, first traveled to the kingdom of Srivijaya in Southeast Asia to learn Sanskrit. He then took passage on a merchant ship to India. Like Faxian, Yijing was interested in monastic rules. In fact, one of the main reasons for his trip was to rectify what he calls the "errors" in the applications of the "original Buddhist principles" in China. In his travelog, entitled *The Record of Buddhism as Practiced in India Sent Home from the Southern Seas*, he describes forty practices at Indian monasteries, ranging from "cleansing after meals" to the "regulations for ordination," and compares them to the procedures observed at monasteries in his homeland.

These pilgrims and hundreds like them brought various kinds of Buddhist accoutrements with them when they returned to China. The relics of the Buddha and Buddhist statutes, texts, and so forth that they brought were often displayed at prominent monasteries and other Buddhist sites to attract monks, lay believers, and other members of society.

Additionally, these Buddhist paraphernalia, some brought by the pilgrims and others supplied by traders, were important in that they helped to re-create in China a Buddhist world where the followers could perform

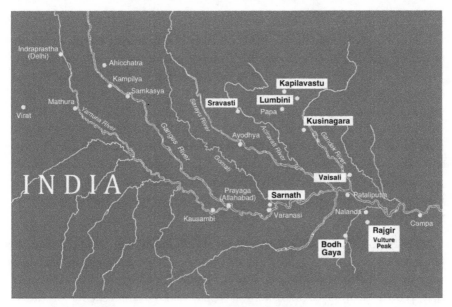

Map 4.4. Buddhist pilgrimage sites in India. (After Sen 2006.)

Figure 4.2. Buddhist site on Mount Wutai, as depicted on a wall-painting at Dunhuang. (After Sen 2003.)

pilgrimages without embarking on the arduous journey to southern Asia. The Chinese clergy was able to establish several Buddhist pilgrimage sites by using such paraphernalia and creating local legends about the sacredness of these places. One example of such a site in China is Mount Wutai (Five Terraces) in Shanxi Province.

Starting sometime in the sixth century, the Buddhist clergy in China began to promote Mount Wutai as the abode of the bodhisattva of wisdom, Manjusri. This was done by manipulating Buddhist texts translated into Chinese, by producing "apocryphal" texts—works that were considered spurious and not originating in India—that emphasized this lore, and by re-creating an Indian world on the mountain using Buddhist artifacts brought from India. The effort was so successful that monks from neighboring regions and even southern Asia started making pilgrimages to the site in order to pay homage to Manjusri. Clearly, the mountain had been transformed into a legitimate Buddhist site, and China, by the eighth century, had emerged as a vital Buddhist realm.

The establishment of Chinese schools of Buddhism, including the Tiantai, Huayan, and Chan (Zen), accompanied the emergence of major pilgrimage sites in China such as Mount Wutai. These Buddhist schools, although they rooted themselves in canonical texts, had no antecedents in India. Their founders, concerned with the validity, complexity, and sometimes the contradictory nature of teachings contained in the translated texts, attempted to synthesize Indian teachings according to the needs of Chinese society. The founder of the Tiantai school, Zhiyi, for example, in an attempt to address the issue of distinct doctrines in the Buddhist texts coming from southern Asia, taught that all such texts, irrespective of their doctrinal orientation, contained the true teachings of the Buddha.

Teachings such as this, which underscored the needs of Chinese Buddhist adherents, are also found in texts composed in China. These so-called apocryphal or indigenous works combined Buddhist teachings with Chinese beliefs and religious motifs and played an important role in the propagation of practices and rituals associated with death and the afterlife. The means to escape purgatory and achieve rebirth in a Buddhist paradise, presented within Confucian views on filial piety but framed in the context of Buddhist teachings on fate and retribution, were common themes in such texts.

Monks from neighboring kingdoms in Japan and Korea, as described below, found the Buddhist centers and pilgrimage sites more accessible and convenient places to visit than those in southern Asia. By the eighth century, China had emerged as a center for disseminating Buddhist ideas and texts. The decline of some of the urban centers of Buddhism in southern Asia and the evolution of South Asian Buddhism toward more esoteric practices also contributed to the establishment of China as an alternate site for the dissemination of Buddhist doctrines. In fact, the Buddhist world in Asia in the eighth and ninth centuries witnessed the emergence of multiple core regions: China, Tibet, and Sri Lanka. Each of these core regions formed their unique networks of exchange. Thus, the Buddhist centers in China were intimately linked to Japan, Korea, and Vietnam; those in Tibet to eastern India and Central Asia; and those in Sri Lanka to Myanmar and the island states in Southeast Asia.

The Tang period (618–907) is usually described as the high point and final phase of the development of Buddhism in China. Buddhism supposedly declined after the Tang dynasty and was replaced by a new form of Confucianism known as neo-Confucianism (discussed in chapter 5). It is true that Buddhism may have reached its high point under the Tang dynasty, especially during the reign of Empress Wu Zetian (r. 690–705). Already, as the wife of Emperor Gaozong (r. 646–83), Empress Wu had exerted her power at the Tang court by removing other wives and concubines of the Tang ruler. In 674, soon after Emperor Gaozong became seriously ill, Wu Zetian created the special title of Heavenly Empress for herself. When the emperor died, she emerged as the de facto ruler. In 690, she declared the founding of a new dynasty known as the

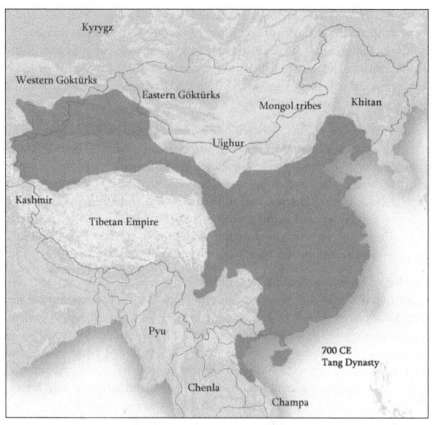

Map 4.5. The Tang dynasty.
(http://en.wikipedia.org/wiki/File:Tang_Dynasty_circa_700_CE.png)

Zhou and took the title Holy and Divine Emperor, the first and only female emperor in Chinese history.

Wu Zetian used Buddhism, as emperors Wu of the Liang dynasty and Yang of the Sui had done before her, to legitimize her rule. She was involved in the fabrication of a Buddhist text that portrayed her as Maitreya, the future Buddha. Her support of the Buddhist community and the ceremonies she sponsored were important factors in making her reign the pinnacle of Buddhism in the history of China. However, this extravagant support subsided soon after the death of Wu Zetian and the restoration of the Tang dynasty. In fact, one of the later rulers, Emperor Wuzong (r. 841–46), launched an unprecedentedly devastating persecution of Buddhism in 845. Known as the Huichang Suppression (after the name of the reign period during which it occurred), the property of Buddhist temples and monasteries was seized, monks were defrocked, and ceremonies and rituals worshiping the Buddha were banned.

The Huichang Suppression was triggered by economic rather than religious motives. By the ninth century, Buddhist temples and monastic institutions had become places of immense wealth, accumulated through donations and because of their tax-exempt status. The collapse of the Tang economy in the second half of the eighth century made the Buddhist institutions a target for court officials and Confucian scholars. Although the Huichang Suppression had a considerable impact on Buddhist institutions and clergy, it by no means led to the disappearance of Buddhism in China. In the eleventh century, Chinese Buddhist practices such as Chan meditation and devotion to the Buddha of the Pure Land reemerged and continued to play a significant role in China. And, as we shall see, Buddhism and Buddhist appurtenances were important elements in diplomatic exchanges between the Song dynasty and neighboring kingdoms.

BUDDHIST NETWORKS IN CHINA AND NEIGHBORING REGIONS

The establishment of Buddhism in China had a significant impact on cross-cultural interactions across the Asian continent. As Buddhist doctrines spread from China to Korea and Japan, almost the whole of Asia, from Iran to Japan, became connected through Buddhist networks of exchange. These networks, overland and maritime, featured not only missionary and pilgrimage activities related to Buddhism but also the transmission of artistic and scientific ideas, mercantile exchanges, and the spread of various cultural elements such as music, dance, and art. These Buddhist networks were instrumental in connecting China to other societies in Asia and in fostering religious, economic, and cultural exchanges with them.

The overland networks of Buddhism linked the Buddhist sacred sites in southern Asia to China through Central Asia and after the fifth century incorporated Korea and Japan. Merchants and Buddhist monks belonging to various ethnic groups traveled through these networks to either trade commodities or proselytize the teachings of the Buddha. These pathways, popularly known as the Silk Roads, witnessed the development of a number of oasis states that became important centers of Buddhism. Khotan, on the southern rim of the Taklamakan Desert, and Kucha, on the northern rim, for example, facilitated Buddhist interactions between China and southern Asia. Dunhuang, another oasis center east of the Taklamakan, became a hub for the Buddhist faithful coming from China and southern Asia. It is now

Figure 4.3. Sogdians depicted on a Chinese stele.
(http://en.wikipedia.org/wiki/File:SogdiansNorthern
QiStellae550CE.jpg.)

renowned for its stunning painted Buddhist caves and the discovery of Buddhist manuscripts in different Asian languages. Dunhuang exemplified the multicultural nature of the transmission of Buddhism and cross-cultural interactions between China and the rest of Asia that took place through Buddhism. There were Chinese clergy and Buddhist novices who learned the teachings of the Buddha, South and Central Asian missionaries who took up residence at the site, and Sogdian merchants, from the Central Asian country of Sogdiana, who formed their guild at this place.

These Central Asian oasis states not only acted as sources for Buddhist teachings for monks and monasteries in China, but they also became important commercial centers and strategic military sites for some of the Chinese dynasties. The Tang dynasty, as was the case with the powerful Han empire, occupied and extended its rule well into the western parts of the Taklamakan Desert. This military occupation by the Tang court facilitated the spread of Chinese Buddhist ideas and art forms to the Central Asian oasis states. The establishment of the Tang empire also contributed to the transmission of other religious traditions, including Manichaeism and Nestorian Christianity, to China through the existing Buddhist networks. Thus, the Buddhist networks not only functioned as conduits for the spread of Buddhist ideas and goods; they also facilitated commercial activity and the transmission of other religious beliefs into China.

After the middle of the eighth century, the Tibetans started exerting dominance over a number of Central Asian oasis states. And at the same time, Islamic forces began occupying the western parts of Central Asia and northwestern India. This disruption of overland Buddhist networks through Central Asia was only temporary. In the tenth century, Tibet emerged as an important Buddhist center, with intimate contacts with monasteries in eastern and northern India. At the same time, rulers of some of the seminomadic tribes occupying northern parts of China, such as the Khitans (Liao, 960–1125) and Tanguts (Xi Xia, 1038–1227), started using Buddhism to legitimize their rule. Kingdoms in Korea and Japan were also closely connected to these revitalized, and in some cases new, networks of Buddhist exchanges. Consequently, in the beginning of the second millennium new Buddhist networks continued to sustain cross-cultural links between northern and eastern India and China, extending to Korea, Japan, Tibet, and Central Asia.

Figure 4.4. Manichaean deities from Turfan. (http://en.wikipedia.org/wiki/File:Manicheans.jpg.)

The fact that the Chinese dynasties continued to be linked to these Buddhist networks can be discerned from the Song court's diplomatic exchanges with its neighbors. Diplomatic intercourse among various states through Buddhism was a common feature along these networks at least since the middle of the first millennium. Chinese dynasties and foreign kingdoms often exchanged Buddhist texts and relics as gifts to the ruler. Some foreign kingdoms sent Buddhist monks as part of their diplomatic entourages to the Chinese courts. Even the Tang court is known to have sent Buddhist monks on special missions to pilgrimage sites in India in order to perform rituals on behalf of the emperor. Perhaps the most noteworthy item on the Buddhist agenda in the diplomatic missions from the Tang court to southern Asia was the procurement of sugar-making technology. Tang sources indicate that in 645 Emperor Taizong sent Buddhist monks along with a diplomatic mission to find and bring to China Indian experts who could manufacture sugar from sugarcane. The fact that they were able to procure the technology can be discerned from a manuscript

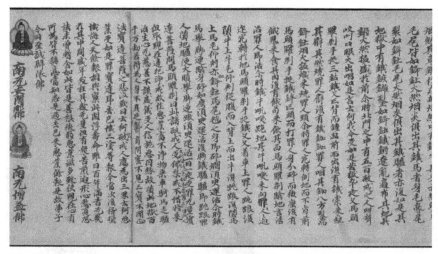

Figure 4.5. Dunhuang manuscript. (© Trustees of the British Museum.)

found in Dunhuang that details the manufacturing process. Sugar, in its liquid form, was at this time in China used mostly for Buddhist rituals. Later it became an important ingredient in Chinese cuisine.

During the Song dynasty, the use of Buddhism in diplomatic exchanges increased significantly. A key reason for this seems to have been growth in the demand for Buddhist paraphernalia by the newly established states of seminomadic peoples such as the Khitans and Tanguts. In fact, this period witnessed the emergence of several Buddhist states in East Asia, including those in Korea, Japan, and southeastern China, some of which competed militarily but were unified culturally through Buddhism. Militarily weak and willing to negotiate peace treaties with these neighboring states, the Song court often offered Buddhist items as diplomatic presents to their rulers. Such use of Buddhism in diplomatic exchanges between the imperial Chinese court and neighboring kingdoms continued during the Mongol Yuan and later periods.

Like the overland routes, the maritime Buddhist networks were involved in diplomatic and commercial exchanges between various regions. They, too, played a significant role in the transmission of cultural and scientific ideas. But, while the overland Buddhist networks mostly became a conduit for the transmission of Mahayana teachings, Theravada doctrines became prevalent along the maritime networks across the Bay of Bengal to the South China Sea. Thus, in Sri Lanka, Myanmar, and most parts of Southeast Asia, Theravada Buddhism became the dominant doctrine.

Some scholars have argued that the transmission of Buddhism from southern Asia to China could have taken place initially through the maritime route.[1] The basis for this argument is evidence from the coastal regions of China, including that from Mount Kongwang, located in the eastern coastal province of Jiangsu. As mentioned in chapter 3, engraved on boulders on the mountain are images of the Buddha and worshippers that date from the late second century. Later, during the third and fourth centuries, South Asian monks are reported to have reached present-day Guangzhou on mercantile ships, where they established some of the earliest Buddhist monasteries in the area. These included the famous Guangxiao Monastery, founded by Tanmoyeshe (Dharmayasas), a monk from Kapisa in present-day Afghanistan-Pakistan.

The intimate connection between seafaring merchants and the Buddhist community also can be discerned from the biography of the renowned Sogdian monk Kang Senghui. Kang's ancestors (who would ultimately have hailed from western Central Asia) lived in India and engaged in commercial activities. To establish a commercial venture, his father migrated to Jiaozhi (present-day Vietnam), where Kang grew up and became a Buddhist monk. In 247, Kang arrived in what is now the city of Nanjing and propagated Buddhism under the ruler Sun Quan. His story suggests the possible transmission of Buddhism from Jiaozhi in Southeast Asia to China through the maritime route. Southeast Asia was also a transit point for Buddhist monks traveling between China and southern Asia. Faxian was perhaps the first Chinese pilgrim to make this trip, sometime in 409. He first traveled on a mercantile ship from the port of Tamralipti in eastern India to Sri Lanka and then, after a two-year stay, boarded a seagoing vessel for China. The ship passed the island of Sumatra, where, according to Faxian, Buddhism had not yet been established.

However, when Yijing traveled to southern Asia through the maritime route in the seventh century, the kingdom of Srivijaya on Sumatra had emerged as a leading Buddhist center. As noted earlier, Yijing stayed on the island for six months to learn Sanskrit before proceeding to southern Asia. In contrast to many other sites in Southeast Asia, Mahayana Buddhism was the prevalent form of Buddhism in Srivijaya, where there were monasteries with large numbers of monks. In the tenth and eleventh centuries, even monks from southern Asia went to Srivijaya to study Buddhism. The most famous was Atisa Dipankara (980–1054), who, in the early eleventh century, studied Buddhism in Srivijaya for twelve years before going to Tibet. Atisa's Buddhist studies in Sumatra and later propagation of the faith in Tibet points to the intertwined nature of the maritime and overland networks of Buddhist exchanges that was already evident in the fifth century when Faxian traveled to southern Asia by the overland route and returned by the maritime route. At the time of Faxian's pilgrimage, southern Asia was considered to be the central realm of Buddhism, the source of all Buddhist teachings. When Atisa ventured from southern Asia to Sumatra and then to Tibet it was clear that there were multiple centers of Buddhist learning that interacted with each other through the transmission of doctrines and exchanges of religious goods. During the Mongol Yuan period, Qubilai Khan (r. 1260–94) is reported to have shared an interest with the ruler of the Persian Ilkhanate in procuring Buddhist relics from southern Asia. In the 1270s and 1280s, Qubilai sent several embassies to Sri Lanka and southern India to bring relics of the Buddha to China. Even Marco Polo allegedly saw the Buddhist relics that Qubilai brought from southern Asia. The Buddhist networks that earlier linked China to the rest of Asia continued to exist at least until the thirteenth century.

The intertwined nature of overland and maritime Buddhist networks can also be seen in the spread of the doctrine from China to Korea and Japan. In the fourth century, Buddhism spread from China to Korea via the overland routes. It was soon accepted by the three kingdoms, Koguryo, Paekche (18 BCE–660 CE), and Silla (57 BCE–938 CE), that then ruled the Korean Peninsula. Almost two centuries later, King Seong (r. 523–54) of Paekche introduced the religion into Japan by sending Buddhist monks to the Japanese court in Nara through the sea route. The spread of Buddhism to Korea and Japan triggered the formation of distinct Buddhist networks between these two regions and China.

For monks from Korea and Japan, China was the main source of Buddhist doctrines and pilgrimage activity. Only on a few occasions did Korean and Japanese monks visit the Indian subcontinent to procure Buddhist texts or pay homage to the Buddha. Won-hyo (617–86) and Uisang (625–702) from Korea and Kukai (774–835), Ennin (793–864), and Jojin (1011–81) from Japan traveled to China to learn Buddhist doctrines under famous Chinese monks and returned to their respective kingdoms to establish their own unique schools of Buddhism. Some were able to study with monks from southern Asia residing in China. In the ninth century Kukai, for example, studied Sanskrit under the Gandharan monk Prajna at the Ximing Monastery in the Tang capital. Others, such as the Korean monk Hyecho (704–87), made pilgrimages to India and, instead of returning to their homelands, settled in China to undertake the translation of Buddhist texts.

A number of Japanese monks traveled to China together with the diplomatic missions sent to the Chinese courts as part of official delegations. Often Buddhist monks from Korea and Japan would travel to pilgrimage sites in China associated with Buddhism. While Korean monks regularly visited Mount Jiuhua in present-day Anhui Province, where the body of a Korean prince called Kim Kyogak (630–729) supposedly was transformed into the bodhisattva Ksitigarbha, the Japanese preferred to visit Mount Wutai, which was associated with Manjusri. At the same time as the Korean and Japanese monks imported Buddhist teachings from China, they also modified these teachings to fit their own cultural setting, similar to what the Chinese had done with regard to Indian beliefs. In addition, the two regions established Buddhist pilgrimage sites within their respective borders to transform their lands from peripheries into central realms of Buddhism.

In sum, the Buddhist networks across Asia that emerged in the second century gradually connected China to various parts of Asia. These networks facilitated the formation of a unique relationship with southern Asia that centered on the transmission of Buddhist doctrines, the exchange of religious goods, and diplomatic and technological exchanges inspired by Buddhism. In the same way, the Buddhist

Figure 4.6. The bodhisattva Ksitigarbha. (© Trustees of the British Museum.)

networks that linked China to Central Asia, Southeast Asia, and Japan and Korea contributed to and sustained cultural and political exchanges. In other words, Buddhist networks were instrumental in fostering China's interactions with foreign societies; they brought about tremendous social and cultural changes within China and also contributed to the spread of beliefs and ideas formulated in China to other societies in Asia.

5

Chına ın the Age of Commerce

The middle of the eighth century marked a watershed for the commercial policies and economic structures in China. The rigid system of controlling and limiting commercial activities to designated sites, especially beyond the confines of the city gates, and the low status conferred on merchants due to Confucian antipathy toward profit-oriented trade rapidly changed after the so-called An Lushan rebellion. In 755, a Sogdian-Turkish general in the Tang army named An Lushan (703?–57) rebelled and fought a devastating war against the Tang court that lasted eight years. While in 763 the Tang armies (with the help of Uyghur allies) were eventually able to quell An Lushan's rebellion and destroy the Yan dynasty (756–59) he had founded, it left the Tang empire in a deep financial crisis.

To recuperate from the financial catastrophe, the Tang court instituted several measures to revive the economy and rebuild the empire. These measures, as this chapter outlines, not only triggered rapid growth in commercial activity within China, but they also led to the intensification of the region's economic interactions with foreign kingdoms. The latter development was also facilitated by the formation of Muslim trading networks that connected China to the Persian Gulf and beyond. Because of these two developments, China rapidly emerged as one of the main destinations for traders around the world. In fact, in the twelfth and thirteenth centuries, with increased demand for its bulk goods and porcelain, China exerted significant influence on the world economy.

Another noteworthy change after the mid-eighth century was the emergence of maritime routes as the main conduits of commercial exchanges between China and the rest of the world. The Song, Yuan, and Ming dynasties, which succeeded the Tang, paid considerable attention to developing shipbuilding technologies and maritime ties with the outside world. As a result, traders from China started venturing into the Indian Ocean and forming their own mercantile networks. The entry of the Chinese into the Indian Ocean networks culminated in the grand maritime voyages of Admiral Zheng He, marking the cultural, economic, and political dominance of the Ming court in the early-fifteenth-century maritime world.

Finally, the latter half of the eighth century also witnessed the revival of Confucianism, with new philosophical ideas, some of which were influenced by Buddhism. The latter religion, as noted in chapter 4, was by the Song period thoroughly transformed into a Chinese religion and continued to exert significant influence on the lives of the common people and folk traditions. But this revived Confucianism, usually known in the West as neo-Confucianism, not only influenced the intellectual and social lives of those living in China but also significantly impacted Korea and Japan.

THE CONFUCIAN REVIVAL

The foundations of the Confucian revival already had been laid in the Tang, with the xenophobic (antiforeign) reaction to Buddhism of scholars such as Han Yu (768–824) and more thoughtful critiques by thinkers such as Li Ao (774–836). The revival of Confucianism, however, was not simply a matter of more or less violent xenophobia but was also the reflection of an inevitable response to the manifestly powerful and attractive features of Buddhism that were lacking in Confucianism. Among the transformations that resulted were the development of meditationlike "quiet sitting," the remaking of *li* (principle) into a transcendental concept, and the reshaping of the Confucian sage from a person of great wisdom and virtue into a spiritual paragon of deep, subjective insight deriving from rigorous self-cultivation. Thus, essential features of Buddhism were incorporated into the neo-Confucianism that emerged during the transition from the Tang to the Song.

In the early Song period, the leading neo-Confucians were Zhou Dunyi (1017–73), a specialist on the *Yijing* (Book of Changes), and Shao Yong (1011–77), who refashioned Daoist diagrams pertaining to immortality into cosmological explanations of Confucian philosophy. Their contemporary, Zhang Zai (1020–77), who had devoted lengthy study to Buddhism, proposed that everything in the universe is composed of *qi* (material energy) in accordance with *taiji* (the great ultimate). Zhang's nephews, Cheng Hao (1032–85) and Cheng Yi (1033–1107), emphasized that all things are informed by *li* (principle), resulting respectively in *xinxue* (study of the heart/mind) and *daoxue* (study of the Way).

The most renowned Song neo-Confucian of all was Zhu Xi (1130–1200), a towering figure who formulated an approach that came to be called *lixue* (study of principle) on the basis of the ideas of his forerunners. Knowledge of Zhu Xi's interpretations of the classics was required for those taking the civil service examinations during succeeding centuries. Although Zhu Xi forged rationality, knowledge, and morality into an integral system of thought and practice, his originally stimulating synthesis became so dogmatically orthodox that a reaction set in against it. One

Maps 5.1A and 5.1B. The Song dynasty: (A) Northern Song (above); and (B) Southern Song (below). (http://en.wikipedia.org/wiki/File:China_11a.jpg and http://en.wikipedia.org/wiki/File:China_11b.jpg.)

of Zhu Xi's sharpest opponents was Wang Yangming (1472–1529), who stressed introspection and intuition, so much so that his opponents referred to him as a "crypto-Buddhist."

Neo-Confucianism also had a powerful impact on Japan and Korea. Indeed, it was the official guiding philosophy of Japan's Tokugawa period (1603–87). It is interesting that, prior to this time, Confucian studies had been kept alive in Japan primarily by Buddhist clerics. During the Tokugawa period, however, Confucianism emerged from the shadow of Buddhism and found a voice of its own, with Japanese scholars favoring Wang Yangming's ideas almost as much as those of Zhu Xi. Under the Tokugawa *bakufu* (the collective officialdom of the ruling shogunate), neo-Confucianism contributed to the transformation of the sociopolitical order from one of feudal dominance to one that more readily permitted organization by group and class. Yet this did not lead to the replacement of Japanese social norms by Chinese values. For example, in China soldiers were held in low esteem, but in Japan warriors (samurai) retained their old aristocratic respect. Nonetheless, with the new ethical humanism fostered by neo-Confucianism, the influential doctrine of *kokugaku* (national learning) arose. Thus, the foundations of Japan's early modern political philosophy were heavily imbued with neo-Confucian precepts.

The situation was similar in Korea, with Confucianism initially in a secondary position to Buddhism. Already by the early part of the Choson dynasty (1392–1910), however, neo-Confucianism had become the dominant intellectual system among the *yangban* (Korea's landed aristocratic class) of scholars and military men. Schools flourished, libraries were amassed, and artists were supported—all espousing Confucian ideals. Under the great king Sejong (r. 1418–50), who created the Korean alphabet (*hangul*) in order to make learning more accessible to the people, neo-Confucian thought was actively promoted and the classics assiduously studied. Although Buddhism apparently was permitted to exist outside of the main political centers, some historians hold that it experienced extreme repression during the Choson dynasty, which strongly favored neo-Confucianism. This even had a negative effect on tea drinking in Korea, since it was perceived to be closely linked to Buddhism. The Koreans, in fact, were such enthusiastic supporters of neo-Confucianism during this period that they preserved Confucian temple rituals and music better than did the Chinese, who in modern times have traveled to Korea to observe aspects of Confucianism that had disappeared in China so that they could reconstruct them in their homeland.

ECONOMIC CHANGES AND MUSLIM NETWORKS

We must now step back in time to the middle of the Tang period to examine the fundamental causes of the massive economic transformation that occurred in China and beyond during the succeeding centuries.

An Lushan's rebellion against the Tang dynasty in the middle of the eighth century seems to have been instigated primarily by rivalry among the Tang generals and because of An's aspiration to acquire a higher position at the court. With his powerful rebel forces, An Lushan was able to defeat the

Tang army and swiftly capture Luoyang, the spiritual capital of the dynasty. His troops also entered the Tang administrative capital Chang'an, forcing the reigning emperor, Xuanzong, to flee to Sichuan in southwestern China. In 756, An Lushan founded the Yan dynasty and declared himself the new emperor. Within a year, however, he was assassinated by his son and heir, An Qingxu, who in turn was killed by Shi Shiming, a subordinate of An Lushan, in 759. Shi Shiming assumed the title of emperor but could only sustain opposition to the Tang for two more years. He was killed in a plot hatched by his oldest son, and with his death the Yan dynasty collapsed, bringing to an end one of the most devastating rebellions in Chinese history.

While the armies loyal to the Tang court were able to quell the rebellion and recapture the lost territories, it was evident that powerful generals and governors across Tang China were able to exert more power and autonomy than before. The economic situation in the aftermath of the rebellion was more disturbing to the Tang court than the autonomy of a few governors. It recognized that in order to restore its diminishing financial resources it had to institute new economic policies. It soon enacted a decentralized taxation system known as the *liangshui fa* (twice-yearly tax), under which local provinces were authorized to collect taxes and give a fixed amount of revenue to the central government. Taxpayers had the option of paying taxes during either of the two collection cycles within a year with cash or in kind. The court also overhauled the market system by allowing traders to set up stalls within city walls and at any time during the day. These steps contributed to the emergence of active private entrepreneurs, stimulated commercial exchanges, and led to an increase in revenue for the central government.

The Tang court also established a special office, known as the Shibosi (Bureau of Maritime Commerce), to oversee maritime commerce at Guangzhou, where traders from the Persian Gulf and South and Southeast Asia had been trading with local merchants. The court-appointed head of this office was charged with responsibilities that included levying duties on imported goods, the management of foreign diasporic communities, and the administration of trade between Chinese and foreign merchants. This seems to have been the first time that the fiscal benefit of administrating maritime trade was recognized by a court in China.

This new interest in administrating maritime trade coincided with the formation of Islamic trading networks, which significantly bolstered commerce between China and the Persian Gulf. *Akhbar al-Sin wa'l-Hind* (An Account of China and India), compiled around 851 and attributed to a merchant called Sulayman, and *Kitab al-Masalik wa'l-Mamalik* (Book of

Highways and Kingdoms), written by Ibn Khurdadhbih, record the voyages of Muslim seafaring merchants from the Arabian port of Siraf through Sri Lanka and India to Guangzhou. According to the former work, Guangzhou was a "haven for boats and a market-place of Arab and Chinese commerce," where "a Muslim is made an arbitrator by the ruler of China to settle the disputes arising among the Muslims visiting this region; this is what the King of China desires" (Ahmed 1989: 37). The commentator of the second text, a person named Abu Zayd, points out that in 878 a rebel force under Huang Chao massacred thousands of foreign merchants, including Muslims and Jews, which is corroborated by Chinese texts. This report suggests the existence of large numbers of foreign traders who had settled at the Guangzhou port expressly to trade with Tang China.

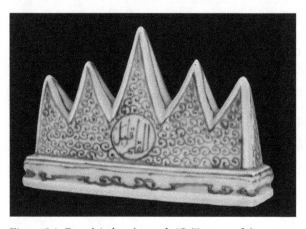

Figure 5.1. Porcelain brush stand. (© Trustees of the British Museum.)

While merchants from different parts of the world arrived at the coastal regions of China to profit from the liberalized commercial policies of the Tang government, Muslim traders of diverse ethnic backgrounds established their vast trading networks across the Indian Ocean. By the late tenth century these merchants were actively transporting Chinese silk and porcelain through Southeast Asia and the coastal regions of India and Sri Lanka to the Persian Gulf. From the Persian Gulf they brought aromatics and other goods to Chinese markets. Their role in the foreign trade of China, as noted below, increased significantly during the Song dynasty.

In addition to the fiscal changes instituted by the late Tang court, China witnessed several other significant developments in the tenth and eleventh centuries that stimulated the economy of the region. New varieties of crops were introduced from Southeast Asia, knowledge of improved irrigation machinery and techniques spread throughout China because of the development of wood-block printing, and large numbers of settlers from other parts of China started migrating toward the fertile southern regions. As a result of these developments, the population of China during the Song dynasty grew almost

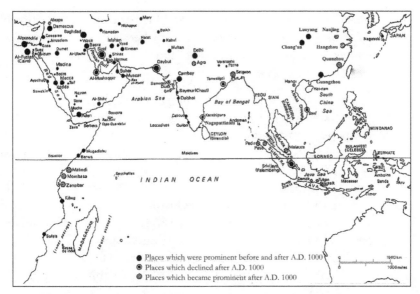

Map 5.2. Medieval Asian ports and cities, ca. 1000 CE. (After Sen 2003.)

fourfold from 32 million in 961 to about 121 million in 1109. The growth in population had a considerable impact on city structure, mercantile activity, and the legal system. At the same time, however, the emergence of powerful seminomadic adversaries in the north posed a military threat to the Song government, which was established in Kaifeng in 960. During the late tenth century and the first half of the eleventh, the Song lost several key battles with the Khitans and Tanguts, which resulted in the signing of peace treaties and the payment of large amounts of silver, silk, and tea to their adversaries. In 1004–5, the Song court, for example, was forced to sign the Shanyuan treaty with the Khitans, under which the Song government paid an annual tribute of 100,000 taels of silver and 200,000 bolts of silk to the Khitans. The 1044 treaty with the Tanguts required the Song court to send an annual tribute of 50,000 taels of silver, 130,000 bolts of silk, and 10,000 catties of tea.[1]

The economic burden of these peace treaties compelled the Song court to explore its maritime frontiers for possible financial resources. It established new customhouses at port cities, instituted new laws and policies to facilitate internal and external commerce, developed a credit system for itinerant traders, and actively invited foreign seafaring merchants to visit the ports and markets of China. One of the ministers pushing for fiscal reforms at the Song court was Wang Anshi (1021–86), who not only put forth proposals to liberalize and facilitate commercial activity but also took steps to monetize the economy and revamp the educational system to train good administrators. These measures led to rapid growth in government revenue and further commercialization of the society. Maritime trade, in particular, not only became a source of income for the government but also led a significant number of people to settle in the coastal regions of China.

Also benefiting from these policies of the Song court were foreign merchants, especially Muslim traders, who by this time had established extensive diasporic communities and commercial networks throughout the Indian Ocean and beyond, including at the leading Chinese port called Quanzhou (Zayton in Western sources). These Muslim traders not only traded goods at Chinese markets, but they also were intimately involved in the tribute system, which for the first time in Chinese history was formally recognized as a source of government revenue. In fact, the Song court offered incentives, including tax breaks and return gifts, to the tribute carriers. In return, the court acquired foreign commodities without payment, which it sold on the open market for huge profits. Muslim traders exploited this new system in various ways. They often appeared at the Song court as official representatives of non-Islamic foreign kingdoms such as the Cholas of southern India and Srivijaya in Southeast Asia. Some of these merchants received honorary titles for their contributions in bringing tribute to the Song court.

The changes in economic policies and structures that began during the late Tang period profoundly altered the nature of foreign trade between China and the rest of the world. While during earlier periods luxury goods, such as rhinoceros horns, beads, and glassware, formed the main components of foreign trade, during the Song dynasty there was a shift toward bulk goods such as black pepper, cardamom, gharuwood, and frankincense, which were used for cuisine, medicine, and making incense. Some of these commodities originated in the Middle East and were supplied to the Chinese by Muslim merchants. But Muslim traders were also active in southern and Southeast Asia. These commercial bases facilitated the purchase and sale of Chinese goods in markets in the Middle East and the Mediterranean region.

Although maritime trade became increasingly vibrant during the Song period, commercial activity across the overland routes through Central Asia also continued. The newly established seminomadic states formed by the Khitans and Tanguts traded with Song China as well as kingdoms in the western parts of Central Asia. The Tibetans, on the other hand, were involved in an extensive horse and tea trading relationship with Song China. The tributary exchanges between the Song and the overland kingdoms show the same commercial patterns as do the exchanges coming to China via the maritime routes in that all of them were commercially motivated. Indeed, the period between the

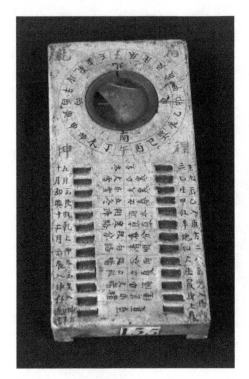

Figure 5.2. Chinese compass. (© Trustees of the British Museum.)

tenth and thirteenth centuries was marked by an upsurge in trading activity from East Asia to the Mediterranean region. Some have referred to this period as the age of global commerce, with demand at Song markets as the driving force for cross-regional trading activity.

The extensive trading activity during the Song dynasty facilitated the development of several technologies in China. The Song period, which is marked in general by the emergence of new technologies such as movable type printing and the use of gunpowder, also witnessed significant progress in shipbuilding and navigational techniques. With input from Southeast Asia, the Song shipbuilders started constructing vessels capable of sea voyages. By the end of the twelfth century, these vessels were sailing to Southeast Asia and shortly thereafter to southern Asia. Also available to the Song sailors were compasses, which provided better navigational knowledge.

At the same time, merchants from China started engaging in maritime commerce and forming diasporic communities at major ports in Southeast Asia. Indeed, the latter half of the Song period, which became known as the Southern Song when the capital was moved to Hangzhou due to the occupation of Kaifeng by the Jurchens in 1127, marked the beginnings of Chinese trading networks that quickly overshadowed the Muslim networks of the previous periods.

THE MARITIME WORLD OF CHINA

Advances in shipbuilding and navigational techniques were instrumental in the emergence of the Yuan and Ming dynasties as major naval powers in the Indian Ocean. Chinese traders and mercantile ships from the coastal regions of China and the diasporic communities in Southeast Asia dominated the maritime trading and transportation networks during this period. The

Figure 5.3. Song dynasty ship from Quanzhou.
(http://en.wikipedia.org/wiki/File:Quanzhou_Boat.jpg.)

culmination of Chinese maritime power and its interactions with foreign peoples came with the seven voyages of Admiral Zheng He across the Indian Ocean between 1405 and 1433. After these voyages, however, the Ming court decided to terminate maritime expeditions and limit its exchanges with foreign courts. The scaling back of the naval domination of the maritime world by the Ming court seems to have created a political vacuum in the Indian Ocean that was eventually filled by European commercial enterprises that gradually occupied the major ports and established colonial rule over most of Asia in the eighteenth and nineteenth centuries.

Interest in extending China's supremacy over the maritime world dates from the Mongol Yuan period of Chinese history. The conquests of Genghis Khan (ca. 1162–1227) had laid the foundations for one of the largest empires in world history. Divided into four major entities, the Yuan khanate in China, the Ilkhanate in Persia, the Golden Horde in Europe, and the Chagatai khanate in Central Asia, the descendants of Genghis ruled over large parts of Asia and Europe. Cross-cultural interactions and exchanges within Asia and between Asians and Europeans increased significantly during the Mongol period. Several Europeans, such as John of Plano Carpini, William of Rubruck, and Marco Polo, went to China during this period and wrote detailed accounts of their journeys. Ibn Battuta traveled from northern Africa to the Middle East and southern Asia before making his way to Yuan China. Similarly, diplomats and other travelers from Yuan China visited ports and cities across Asia.

The Mongol conquest of China was accomplished by Qubilai Khan, the grandson of Genghis. In 1279 he routed the last remaining stronghold of the Southern Song dynasty and took control of the lucrative maritime trade in the coastal regions of China. In order to rule over the majority Han Chinese population, Qubilai adopted existing Chinese political ideologies and allowed the populace to maintain its traditional social and cultural structures rather than imposing Mongol customs. While he had a number of Chinese advisers and ministers, Qubilai also employed foreigners from near and far at his court, which was located on the site of present-day Beijing. He also asserted his leadership among other descendants of Genghis by declaring himself the Great Khan, the legitimate heir to Genghis Khan.

This claim by Qubilai to be the Great Khan of the Mongols triggered a civil war among the four khanates, with the Chagatais in Central Asia as his main rival. Because of this rivalry and due to the need to portray himself as the great khan of the entire Mongol empire, Qubilai launched several military offensives against neighboring kingdoms. These included naval raids against Japan in 1274 and 1280 and against Champa and Java in 1281 and 1293, respectively.

Figure 5.4. The Mongol attack on Japan.
(http://en.wikipedia.org/wiki/File:Takezaki_suenaga_ekotoba3.jpg.)

Each of these missions ended in failure, but it was clear that the Yuan court possessed naval forces that could go beyond the maritime frontiers of China, something no previous courts in China had attempted. Also, for the first time in Chinese history, the Yuan court took an active role in dispatching diplomatic envoys to maritime kingdoms in the Indian Ocean. The southern coastal region of India, and the Malabar coast in particular, was a key destination for some of these missions. Apparently the Yuan court perceived the Malabar coast as an important commercial and strategic transit location.

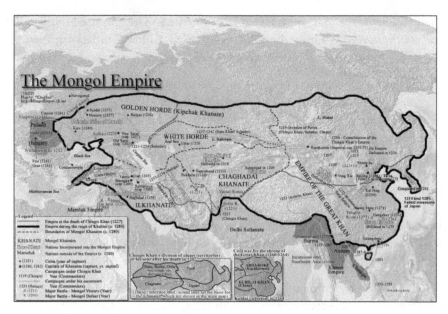

Map 5.3. The Mongol empire.
(http://en.wikipedia.org/wiki/File:Mongols-map.png.)

Indeed, it was not only frequented by Chinese merchants destined for the Persian Gulf but also provided a link to the Ilkhanate, the khanate centered in Persia and an ally of the Yuan court in the Mongol civil war.

The commercial significance of the Malabar coast to the Yuan court and merchants is underscored in the record of a Chinese sailor, Wang Dayuan. Compiled in circa 1333, his *Daoyi zhi lüe* (Brief Record of the Island Foreigners), in addition to detailing the commercial products and activity on the Malabar coast, describes other important ports in Southeast Asia, South Asia, and the Persian Gulf. The work is among the first Chinese records of these ports written from the perspective of a trader. It demonstrates the expansion of the Chinese trading network during the Yuan period and suggests the importance of maritime commerce in China in the fourteenth century.

The vast Chinese maritime networks, the presence of Chinese ships across the Indian Ocean, and the importance of the Malabar coast to the Chinese traders were also noticed by Marco Polo (ca. 1254–1324). This Venetian trader is said to have arrived at the Yuan court sometime around 1275 with his father, Nicolo Polo, and an uncle, Maffeo Polo, both merchants. Marco Polo's record of his travels to Yuan China via the overland route and his return to Venice by sea are included in his book, *Description of the World*. Also found in this work are detailed notices about various Chinese cities and towns and observations of commercial activities within Yuan China and on the overland and maritime routes. The author describes the maritime links between Yuan China and the Indian coast and notes the diplomatic exchanges between the Yuan court and Ilkhanate in Persia. In fact, he reports that the three Polos accompanied an entourage that escorted the Yuan princess Kokachin to Persia, where she was supposed to marry the Ilkhan ruler Arghun.

While Marco Polo's record indicates extensive trading activity between Europe and Yuan China, religious exchanges between the two regions are evidenced in the works of Friar Odoric, of the Franciscan order in Italy, and another Italian Franciscan called John of Montecorvino. Both traveled to China by the maritime route, passing though southern Asia, to proselytize Catholicism in Yuan China. While John of Montecorvino reached China in 1294 and lived there for over twenty years, reportedly succeeding in converting some Chinese to Christianity, Friar Odoric was in Yuan China for only three years, from 1323 to 1326, and had a limited impact on the population.

A large number of Muslims and even some Hindus were living in Yuan China, especially at the port known as Quanzhou. Located in present-day Fujian Province, the port had attracted many foreign traders since the Song period. One Muslim, Pu Shougeng, even served as the administrator of foreign trade under the Song dynasty but changed his allegiance to Qubilai when the Mongol forces were about to enter the town. Mosques and graves built by Muslim settlers dot the port. There are also remains of Christian churches and at least one Hindu temple, most likely built by a Tamil diasporic community.

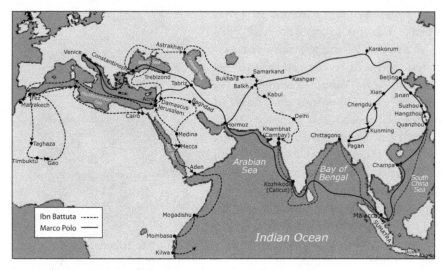

Map 5.4. Marco Polo's and Ibn Battuta's travels to China.

Figure 5.5. A mosque in Quanzhou.
(http://upload.wikimedia.org/wikipedia/
commons/d/db/Mosque_in_Quanzhou%2C_
Fujian%2C_China.jpg.)

The Moroccan traveler Ibn Battuta, who reached the port in 1347 as a representative of the ruler of the Delhi sultanate, noticed Quanzhou's ethnic and religious diversity. Noteworthy in his account of the Chinese port are his meetings with a number of Muslims who frequently traveled between southern Asia and the Chinese port.

Quanzhou was also the port from which Ad-miral Zheng He, the famous Chinese Muslim eunuch, embarked on the first of his seven grand voyages across the Indian Ocean in 1405. Born in 1371 in present-day Yunnan Province in southwestern China, Zheng He belonged to the Muslim Hui ethnic group. His father and grandfather are reported to have made the hajj to Mecca. In 1381, when the Ming forces occupied Yunnan Province, Zheng was captured, castrated, and sent to the capital to serve the Ming ruler Yongle. Zheng He's sea voyages were supported and financed by Yongle, most likely to assert Ming China's cultural and military superiority in the Indian Ocean region. Zheng He's armada, which usually included about twenty-seven thousand people and more than two hundred vessels, did not occupy any of the Indian Ocean kingdoms, but on several occasions he played a role in changing some of their regimes.

Figure 5.6. Tribute of giraffe.
(http://en.wikipedia.org/wiki/
File:ShenDuGiraffePainting.jpg.)

When Zheng He sailed for the first time in 1405, Calicut on the Malabar coast was his main destination. The same appears to have been true of the second and third voyages, all of which did not go beyond southern Asia. Zheng He's fourth voyage, in 1413, reached Oman on the southeast coast of the Arabian Peninsula. The fifth and sixth voyages went farther, to the eastern coastal region of Africa, including the Maldives and Mogadishu. On his seventh and final voyage, Zheng He was involved in a conflict between Cochin and Calicut and probably died on the Malabar coast. His body was reportedly buried at sea. The Yongle emperor had died a few years before Zheng He's seventh trip and, with the death of the admiral, imperial support for the voyages subsided, bringing an end to the maritime voyages and a severe reaction on the part of the Confucian literati against the Ming court's active dealings with faraway foreign kingdoms. Some scholars have suggested that this change in the Ming court's foreign policy resulted in the seclusion and decline of Chinese civilization.

Still, Zheng He's missions accomplished several things. First, they significantly expanded tributary relations between the Ming court and foreign kingdoms. Indeed, during the Yongle period, delegations from forty-six kingdoms are reported to have arrived at the Ming court to pay tribute to the Chinese emperor (Li 2006: 113). Second, the voyages stimulated maritime trade and the establishment of new trading emporia such as Malacca in Southeast Asia and Cochin in southern Asia. Third, they facilitated the spread

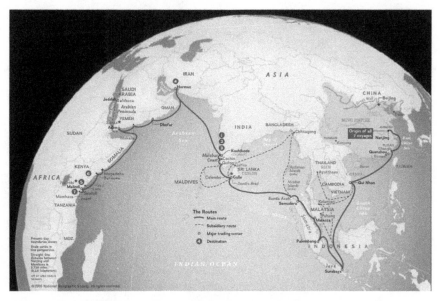

Map 5.5. Zheng He's voyages. (Courtesy of *National Geographic*.)

of Chinese diasporic communities, especially in Southeast Asia. Finally, the Zheng He voyages strengthened and augmented the maritime networks that linked the various Asian ports. This last accomplishment proved beneficial to European commercial enterprises, whose ships traveled through these same networks to colonize most of Asia not long after the Zheng He voyages ended.

CONCLUSION

We have traced the cultural, political, and economic evolution of China from the Neolithic period through the Bronze and Iron ages to the Medieval period, up to the beginning of the European Age of Exploration. Throughout the nearly four millennia of prehistory and history addressed in this study, the fortunes of China have waxed and waned. At times China has been more or less tightly united under the rule of a particular dynasty, and at other times it has been split into two or more (sometimes even ten or more) competing states. Yet, from the latter part of the second millennium BCE onward, there has always been a pattern of centripetal forces drawing China together after forces contributing to disunity have spent themselves.

What were the factors that led to the coherence of China and, in contrast, resulted in the recurrent dissolution of China into a splintered array of warring states?

Many forces held China together, especially a common cosmo-political ideology wherein the ruler constituted the focal power of a supreme deity (*shangdi*) or heaven (*tian*) among men, a socioethical system that elevated ancestors and elders to positions of enormous respect, and a commanding cultural complex that depended on elite mastery of a body of classical texts and the demanding script in which they were written. Above all—particularly after the establishment of the postfeudal Qin-Han bureaucratic empire—was the creation of a small but extremely formidable body of Confucian literati (the *ru*) who both embodied and espoused all of the centralizing tendencies enumerated above. Much of the prestige and power of the literati derived from their monopoly over the full range of the writing system.

Factors that led to the periodic disintegration of China included not only revolts and external invasions but also extraordinary corruption and cruelty on the part of the ruling elites, economic distress, and natural disasters. As often happens in such cases, rebellions would break out in various parts of the realm. The typical leader of such uprisings might be a peasant, visionary, discontented military general, or other aspirant. From whatever walk of life such a man emerged, he might end up as the leader of a local, transitory stronghold or minikingdom that could convulse the entire empire before being subdued. The Turco-Sogdian general An Lushan, who almost ended the reign of Tang rulers in the eighth century, is an example of such a person. A more successful leader of a rebellion might manage to carve out a section of territory as his own dominion, which would last for several generations of heirs, or he might—with good fortune, able associates, and impressive talents—become the founder of a new dynasty. And so the cycle would begin again.

A noteworthy feature of this endless flux between fragmentation and integration is that the leaders who patched up and expanded the empire were, as often as not, themselves of full or partial non-Chinese extraction or relied heavily on collaborators who had such a background. In particular, the skillful mounted warriors from the north and the northwest had an enormous impact on the course of history in China (Mair 2005). This fact alone is testimony to the profoundly intimate linkage between China and the peoples who surrounded it. But the interactions of the inhabitants of China with their neighbors were by no means restricted to war and state formation. As seen repeatedly in these chapters, China was tightly connected to other regions, both near and far, through trading networks, religious ties, and cultural exchanges.

With the European age of global exploration and colonization that commenced around the end of the Ming and the beginning of the Qing, a paradigm shift occurred, and with it came new ideas, new patterns of rulership, and a new sense of belonging and nation. The intellectual, political, and military leaders of the linguistically and ethnically disparate groups that occupied the vast lands of the Manchu (Qing) empire appropriated these new concepts, and thus were born the modern nation of China (Zhongguo) and the Han ethnos.

Precisely how that happened—from the end of the Ming to the beginning of the Republic of China—is the theme of another story. The purpose of this volume has been to demonstrate how, from its very inception as a place of recurring states and enduring traditions, China has never been isolated from other regions of the world. Quite the contrary, China developed as it did over the course of nearly four thousand years because of both its unique geographical circumstances and its interconnectedness with the rest of Eurasia and beyond.

A fallacy of many popular and nationalistic histories (certainly not just of China) is the projection backward in time of current political entities, geographic spreads, and ethnic configurations. Yet, as we have seen from this investigation of the growth and development of China, boundaries are apt to shift and borders are characteristically permeable. What truly persists is an overarching network of human relationships. A brilliant metaphor for this vibrant interconnectedness, well known in traditional China, is the Buddhist philosophical concept of Indra's net, according to which the jewel at each vertex of the net is reflected in all the other jewels of the net.

Today we live within an all-encompassing World Wide Web, which may equally well serve as a metaphor for human integration. The speed of our interactions may have increased enormously, but the essential nature of our interrelatedness persists. As were the ancient Chinese dynasties before the World Wide Web, modern China remains a vital node within the constantly transforming but ever enduring web of human interrelationships.

APPENDIX

SOURCE 1. "The Han Dynasty and Xiongnu," from *Shiji*, Burton Watson translation

SOURCE 2. "Faxian's Pilgrimage to India," from *Foguo ji*, Li Rongxi translation

SOURCE 3. "Record of Mecca by Ma Huan," from *Yingyai Shenglan*, J. V. G. Mills translation

THE HAN DYNASTY AND XIONGNU

The following passage is from the chapter on Xiongnu, the archenemy of the Western Han court, in Shiji *(Records of the Grand Historian), the first Chinese dynastic history compiled by the Han court historians Sima Tan and his son Sima Qian. Under the leader (Shanyu) Maodun, the Xiongnu had defeated the Han armies and imposed a peace treaty that required the Han court not only to pay tribute of valuable goods to the Xiongnu but also to send Chinese imperial princesses as consorts to their leaders.*

From Burton Watson, trans., Records of the Grand Historian: Han Dynasty II, *rev. ed. (Hong Kong and New York: Chinese University of Hong Kong and Columbia University Press, {1961} 1993), 142–45. Used with permission of Columbia University Press.*

Shortly after this, Maodun died and his son Jizhu was set up with the title of Old *Shanyu.* When Jizhu became *Shanyu,* Emperor Wen sent a princess of the imperial family to be his consort, dispatching a eunuch from Yan named Zhonghang Yue to accompany her as her tutor. Zhonghang Yue did not wish to undertake the mission, but the Han officials forced him to do so. "My going will bring nothing but trouble to the Han!" he warned them.

After Zhonghang Yue reached his destination, he went over to the side of the *Shanyu,* who treated him with the greatest favour.

The Xiongnu had always had a liking for Han silks and food stuffs, but Zhonghang Yue told them, "All the multitudes of the Xiongnu nation would not amount to one province in the Han empire. The strength of the Xiongnu lies in the very fact that their food and clothing are different from those of the Chinese, and they are therefore not dependent upon the Han for anything. Now the *Shanyu* has this fondness for Chinese things and is trying to change the Xiongnu customs. Thus, although the Han sends no more than a fifth of its goods here, it will in the end succeed in winning over the whole Xiongnu nation. From now on, when you get any of the Han silks, put them on and try riding around on your horses through the brush and brambles! In no time your robes and leggings will be torn to shreds and everyone will be able to see that silks are no match for the utility and excellence of felt or leather garments. Likewise, when you get any of the Han foodstuffs, throw them away so that the people can see that they are not as practical or as tasty as milk and kumiss!"

He also taught the *Shanyu*'s aides how to make an itemized accounting of the number of persons and domestic animals in the country.

The Han letters addressed to the *Shanyu* were always written on wooden tablets one foot and one inch in length and began, "The emperor respectfully inquires about the health of the great *Shanyu* of the Xiongnu. We send you the following articles, etc., etc." Zhonghang Yue, however, instructed the *Shanyu* to use in replying to the Han a tablet measuring one foot two inches, decorated with broad stamps and great long seals, and worded in the following extravagant manner: "The great *Shanyu* of the Xiongnu, born of Heaven and Earth and ordained by the sun and moon, respectfully inquires about the health of the Han emperor. We send you the following articles, etc., etc."

When one of the Han envoys to the Xiongnu remarked scornfully that Xiongnu custom showed no respect for the aged, Zhonghang Yue began to berate him. "According to Han custom," he said, "when the young men are called into military service and sent off with the army to garrison the frontier, do not their old parents at home voluntarily give up their warm clothing and tasty food so that there will be enough to provide for the troops?"

"Yes, they do," admitted the Han envoy.

"The Xiongnu make it clear that warfare is their business. And since the old and the weak are not capable of fighting, the best food and drink are naturally allotted to the young men in the prime of life. So the young men are willing to fight for the defence of the nation, and both fathers and sons are able to live out their lives in security. How can you say that the Xiongnu despise the aged?"

"But among the Xiongnu," the envoy continued, "fathers and sons sleep together in the same tent. And when a father dies, the sons marry their own stepmothers, and when brothers die, their remaining brothers marry their widows! These people know nothing of the elegance of hats and girdles, nor of the rituals of the court!"

"According to Xiongnu custom," replied Zhonghang Yue, "the people eat the flesh of their domestic animals, drink their milk, and wear their hides, while the animals graze from place to place, searching for pasture and water. Therefore, in wartime the men practise riding and shooting, while in times of peace they enjoy themselves and have nothing to do. Their laws are simple and easy to carry out; the relation between ruler and subject is relaxed and intimate, so that the governing of the whole nation is no more complicated than the governing of one person. The reason that sons marry their stepmothers and brothers marry their widowed sisters-in-law is simply that they hate to see the clan die out. Therefore, although the Xiongnu encounter times of turmoil, the ruling families always manage to stand firm.

In China, on the other hand, though a man would never dream of marrying his stepmother or his brother's widow, yet the members of the same family drift so far apart that they end up murdering each other! This is precisely why so many changes of dynasty have come about in China! Moreover, among the Chinese, as etiquette and the sense of duty decay, enmity arises between the rulers and the ruled, while the excessive building of houses and dwellings exhausts the strength and resources of the nation. Men try to get their food and clothing by farming and raising silkworms and to insure their safety by building walls and fortifications. Therefore, although danger threatens, the Chinese people are given no training in aggressive warfare, while in times of stability they must still wear themselves out trying to make a living. Pooh! You people in your mud huts—you talk too much! Enough of this blabbering and mouthing! Just because you wear hats, what does that make you?"

After this, whenever the Han envoys would try to launch into any sermons or orations, Zhonghang Yue would cut them off at once. "Not so much talk from the Han envoys! Just make sure that the silks and grainstuffs you bring to the Xiongnu are of the right measure and quality, that's all. What's the need for talking? If the goods you deliver are up to measure and of good quality, all right. But if there is any deficiency or the quality is no good, then when the autumn harvest comes we will take our horses and trample all over your crops!"

Day and night he instructed the *Shanyu* on how to manoeuver into a more advantageous position.

FAXIAN'S PILGRIMAGE TO INDIA

In 399, when Faxian embarked on his trip to India, Buddhist doctrines had already taken deep root within Chinese society. However, the rules that govern the monastic institutions had not been properly transmitted to China; also lacking among Chinese Buddhists was detailed knowledge about the Buddhist holy land. Faxian traveled to India by the land route that traversed the Taklamakan Desert and returned to China by the sea route after making a brief stop in Sri Lanka. We are not sure if he was the first Chinese monk to successfully travel to India, but Faxian offered a major contribution in his record of the pilgrimage known as the Foguo ji *(Records of the Buddhist Kingdoms). The work became popular and was widely read. Other authors quoted it frequently, especially those writing about India. Indeed, it was instrumental in creating in China a perception of India as a culturally sophisticated society.*

This passage is from Li Rongxi, trans., "The Journey of the Eminent Monk Faxian," in Lives of Great Monks and Nuns, *BDK English Tripitaka (Berkeley: Numata Center for Buddhist Translation and Research, 2002), 181-82. Used with permission of the Numata Center for Buddhist Translation and Research.*

Going southward from there for eight *yojanas,* Faxian reached the city of Sravasti in the country of Kosala. This city was sparsely populated, having only about two hundred houses. It was once ruled by King Prasenajit. In this city stupas were constructed by people of later times near the ruins of the *vihara* of Mahaprajapati, at the old residence of the elder Sudatta, and at the spot where Angulimala's remains were cremated after he had attained arhatship and entered *parinirvana.* Out of jealousy, the heretical brahmans of the city attempted to demolish these stupas, but the heavens sent thunder and lightning so that they could not destroy the stupas after all.

On the west side of the road, twelve hundred paces from the southern gate of the city, there was a monastery built by the elder Sudatta. Facing east, the door of the monastery was flanked by two stone pillars. The capital of the left pillar was carved in the shape of a wheel, and on the top of the right one stood a statuette of an ox. The water flowing in the stream was clear on both sides of the monastery and there were many trees. Flowers of different colors made the place a lovely sight. This was known as the Jetavana Vihara.

When the Buddha ascended to the Trayastrimsa Heaven to preach the Dharma to his mother for ninety days, King Prasenajit, eager to see his features, had an image of him carved out of oxhead sandalwood and put it on the place where the Buddha usually sat in meditation. When the Buddha returned to the *vihara,* the image left its seat and went out to meet him. The Buddha said to it, "Go back to your seat. After my *parinirvana,* you may serve as a model from which the four groups of my followers can make images." The image returned to the seat. This was the first image ever made of the Buddha, and it served as a model for Buddha images for people of later generations. Then the Buddha moved to a smaller *vihara* twenty paces to the south of the one occupied by the image.

Originally the Jetavana Vihara had seven stories. The kings and people of different countries vied with one another in making offerings to this *vihara.* Silk pennants and canopies were hung in the *vihara,* flowers were scattered, and incense was burned. Lamps were lit every day, [and they burned] continually without interruption. Then it happened that a rat carried off in its mouth the wick of a lamp, which ignited the flowers, pennants, and canopies, and reduced the seven-storied *vihara* to ashes. The kings and the people of different countries lamented and thought that the sandalwood image must also have been consumed by the fire. But four or five days later, when they opened the door of the smaller *vihara* on the east, they discovered, to their great delight, that the image was intact. They rebuilt the *vihara* as a two-story [building] and returned the image to its former place.

Upon arriving at the Jetavana Vihara, Faxian and Daozheng reflected that this was the place where the World-honored One had lived for twenty-five years. They felt sad. They and their friends had been born in a far-off country and had traveled together through many lands, and some had passed away [during the journey]. As they gazed at the place where the Buddha was no more to be seen, they were deeply moved and their hearts were filled with sorrow.

The monks of the *vihara* came out to ask Faxian and his friend, "Where have you come from?"

They replied, "We have come from China."

The monks remarked with amazement, "How wonderful it is that men from a far-off country have come all this way to seek the Dharma!" Then they said among themselves, "None of the teachers in our line of succession has ever seen a Chinese monk come here."

Record of Mecca

The famous Chinese admiral Zheng He was a Muslim and a close confidant of the Ming ruler Yongle. In 1405, with orders from Yongle, Zheng He embarked on the first of his seven voyages across the Indian Ocean. His fleet consisted of over one hundred ships and thousands of crewmembers, including officials, cartographers, geomancers, and soldiers. During the seven voyages, ships from Zheng He's entourage visited all the major ports on the Indian Ocean, from those in the Bay of Bengal region to port towns on the eastern coast of Africa. Zheng He died in 1433 on the Malabar coast of India during his last voyage, and his body seems to have been buried at sea by his crew. Even before Zheng He set out on his seventh and final journey, officials at the Ming court had begun criticizing the expensive and, as they perceived it, meaningless voyages. Imperial support for Zheng He had faded with the death of the Yongle emperor in 1424. After the death of Zheng He, the voyages were discontinued, and, in a severe denunciation of them, the Ming court destroyed the admiral's fleet and burned most of the records and documents collected by the scribes who accompanied him. The following passage is taken from one of the few surviving accounts of the voyages, written by Ma Huan, a Muslim who accompanied Zheng He on three of the seven trips. Ma Huan seems to have reached Mecca, the holy land that Zheng He himself may not have visited.

This passage, with minor stylistic changes, is from J. V. G. Mills, trans., Ma Huan, Ying-Yai Sheng-lan: "The Overall Survey of the Ocean's Shores" [1433] *(Bangkok: White Lotus Press, {1970}, 1997), 173–78. Used with permission of the Hakluyt Society.*

The Country of the Heavenly Square [Mecca]

This country is the country of Moqie (Makka, i.e., Mecca). Setting sail from the country of Guli (Calicut), you proceed towards the south-west—the point *shen* on the compass; the ship travels for three moons, and then reaches the jetty of this country. The foreign name for it is Zhida (Jidda) [and] there is a great chief who controls it. From Zhida you go west, and after travelling for one day you reach the city where the king resides; it is named the capital-city of Moqie.

They profess the Muslim religion. A holy man first expounded and spread the doctrine of his teaching in this country, and right down to the present day the people of the country all observe the regulations of the doctrine in their actions, not daring to commit the slightest transgression.

The people of this country are stalwart and fine-looking, and their limbs and faces are of a very dark purple color.

The menfolk bind up their heads; they wear long garments; [and] on their feet they put leather shoes. The women all wear a covering over their heads, and you cannot see their faces.

They speak the Alabi (Arabic) language. The law of the country prohibits wine-drinking. The customs of the people are pacific and admirable. There are no poverty-stricken families. They all observe the precepts of their religion, and law-breakers are few. It is in truth a most happy country.

As to the marriage- and funeral-rites: they all conduct themselves in accordance with the regulations of their religion.

If you travel on from here for a journey of more than half a day, you reach the Heavenly Hall mosque; the foreign name for this Hall is Kaiabai (Ka'ba). All round it on the outside is a wall; this wall has four hundred and sixty-six openings; on both sides of the openings are pillars all made of white jade-stone; of these pillars there are altogether four hundred and sixty-seven— along the front ninety-nine, along the back one hundred and one, along the left-hand side one hundred and thirty-two, [and] along the right-hand side one hundred and thirty-five.

The Hall is built with layers of five-colored stones; in shape it is square and flat-topped. Inside, there are pillars formed of five great beams of sinking incense wood, and a shelf made of yellow gold. Throughout the interior of the Hall, the walls are all formed of clay mixed with rosewater and ambergris, exhaling a perpetual fragrance. Over [the Hall] is a covering of black hemp-silk. They keep two black lions to guard the door.

Every year on the tenth day of the twelfth moon all the foreign Muslims— in extreme cases making a long journey of one or two years—come to worship inside the Hall. Everyone cuts off a piece of the hemp-silk covering as a memento before he goes away. When it has been completely cut away, the king covers over [the Hall] again with another covering woven in advance; this happens again and again, year after year, without intermission.

On the left of the Hall is the burial-place of Simayi (Isma'il), a holy man; his tomb is all made with green *sabuni* gem-stones; the length is one *zhang* two *chi*, the height three *chi*, and the breadth five *chi*; the wall which surrounds the tomb is built with layers of purple topaz, [and] is more than five *chi* high.

Inside the wall [of the mosque], at the four corners, are built four towers; at every service of worship they ascend these towers, call to the company, and chant the ceremonial. On both sides, left and right, are the halls where all the patriarchs have preached the doctrine; these, too, are built with layers of stone, and are decorated most beautifully.

As to the climate of this place: during [all] the four seasons it is always hot, like summer, and there is no rain, lightning, frost, or snow. At night the dew is very heavy; plants and trees all depend on the dew-water for nourishment; [and] if at night you put out an empty bowl to receive it until day-break, the dew-water will be three *fen* [deep] in the bowl.

As to the products of the land: rice and grain are scarce; [and] they all cultivate such things as unhusked rice, wheat, black millet, gourds, and vegetables. They also have water-melons and sweet melons; [and] in some cases it takes two men to carry each single fruit. Then again they have a kind of tree with twisted flowers, like the large mulberry-tree of the Central Country; it is one or two *zhang* in height; the flowers blossom twice a year; [and] it lives to a great age without withering. For fruits, they have turnips, Persian dates, pomegranates, apples, large pears, and peaches, some of which weigh four or five *jin*.

Their camels, horses, donkeys, mules, oxen, goats, cats, dogs, fowls, geese, ducks, and pigeons are also abundant. Some of the fowls and ducks weigh over ten *jin*.

The land produces rose-water, *anbaer* incense, *qilin,* lions, the "camel-fowl," the antelope, the "fly-o'er-the-grass," all kinds of precious stones, pearls, corals, amber, and other such things.

The king uses gold to cast a coin named a *tangjia*, which is in current use; each has a diameter of seven *fen,* and weighs one *qian* on our official steelyard; compared with the gold of the Central Country it is twenty per cent purer.

If you go west again and travel for one day, you reach a city named Modina (Medina); the tomb of their holy man Mahama (Muhammad) is situated exactly in the city; [and] right down to the present day a bright light rises day and night from the top of the grave and penetrates into the clouds. Behind the grave is a well, a spring of pure and sweet water, named Abi Sansan; men who go to foreign parts take this water and store it at the sides of their ships; if they meet with a typhoon at sea, they take this water and scatter it; [and] the wind and waves are lulled.

In the fifth year of the Xuande [period] an order was respectfully received from our imperial court that the principal envoy the grand eunuch Zheng He and others should go to all the foreign countries to read out the imperial commands and to bestow rewards.

When a division of the fleet reached the country of Guli, the grand eunuch Hong saw that this country was sending men to travel there; whereupon he selected an interpreter and others, seven men in all, and sent them with a load of musk, porcelain articles, and other such things; [and] they joined a ship of this country and went there. It took them one year to go and return.

They bought all kinds of unusual commodities, and rare valuables, *qilin,* lions, "camel-fowls," and other such things; in addition they painted an accurate representation of the "Heavenly Hall"; [and] they returned to the capital.

The king of the country of Moqie also sent envoys who brought some local articles, accompanied the seven men—the interpreter [and others]—who had originally gone there, and presented the articles to the court.

The "facing day" of the autumn moon in [the cyclic year] *xinwei* of the Qingtai [period].

Written by Ma Huan, the mountain-woodcutter of Guiji.[1]

GLOSSARY

An Lushan (703?–757)

A Sogdian general in the Tang army who, in 755, launched a major rebellion against the Tang court. This devastating revolt became known as the An Lushan rebellion.

Apocrypha

Texts that were considered spurious and not included in the Buddhist canon.

arhat

A Buddhist adherent, especially one belonging to the Theravada school, who through discipline and cultivation reaches a high degree of spiritual achievement.

bodhi

The Buddhist idea of awakening to the truth about suffering and its cessation. Also translated as "enlightenment."

bodhisattva

One who has awakened to the wisdom of suffering and its cessation but out of compassion remains in the world to help others attain a similar awakening.

catty

A unit of weight, about 1.5 pounds.

Chan (Zen)

A school of Buddhism that emphasized meditative practices. In Japan it was known as Zen, a name that has been familiar in English for more than half a century. See *dhyana*.

cina-

Literally "of China." A prefix used in Sanskrit for objects that were perceived to have originated in China, such as *cinasi* (hide), *cinamsuka* (silk), *cinka* (camphor), and so on.

cowry/cowrie

Seashell used as currency in China and other parts of Asia.

Dao/Tao

"The Way," the overarching, impersonal, productive force of the universe from which all things are thought to emanate.

daoxue

"Teaching of the Way," the grand synthesis of Confucian thought as propounded chiefly by the great Song neo-Confucian philosopher Zhu Xi.

dhyana

Meditation or meditative practices associated with Buddhism. In Chinese, this is *chan* and in Japanese it is *Zen*.

Die Seidenstrassen

A German word for the "Silk Roads," coined by the geographer Ferdinand von Richthofen in 1877.

Dunhuang

An ancient oasis site in Gansu Province of China where Buddhist monks and traders from various parts of Asia congregated.

Five Pecks of Rice Daoism

Named for the contribution required of its members, this school of Daoism emphasized the correct balance of *qi* and the quest for immortality. It is also known as Tianshi Dao (Way of the Celestial Masters).

hangul

A Korean alphabetic script promulgated in 1446 that eventually replaced Chinese characters used to write Korean.

heqin

Literally "peace and alliance." A strategy by which Chinese courts offered economic incentives and marriage alliances to neighboring states, especially militarily powerful states, in order to maintain peaceful bilateral relations.

Huang-Lao

Considered to be a combination of the tenets of the mythological Yellow Emperor (Huangdi) and the shadowy Laozi (the supposed founder of Daoism), this was a school of thought adhered to by a number of court members during the Western Han dynasty.

Huayan

A Chinese Buddhist school based on Buddhist scripture called *Huayan jing* (Garland Sutra), which emphasized the metaphysical aspects of Buddhism.

Huichang Suppression

One of the most devastating persecutions of Buddhism in China, taking place in 845.

Jataka

Stories of the Buddha's previous births, which highlight the basic teachings of Buddhism.

Ksitigarbha

A popular bodhisattva in East Asia who is considered to be the main exponent of Buddhist teachings before the expected arrival of the future Buddha, Maitreya.

Laozi

The legendary founder of Daoism, who is said to have lived in the sixth or seventh century BCE.

li 禮

In early Confucianism *li* meant rites, rituals, ceremonies, and etiquette.

li 理

Written with a different character from the previous entry, signified the somewhat Buddhicized core concept of the Song Confucians.

liangshui fa

A twice-yearly tax imposed by the Tang court to address the financial crisis triggered by the An Lushan rebellion.

lixue

"The teaching of principle," another name for the neo-Confucian precept and school that was also called *daoxue*.

Madhyadesa

Literally "Middle Country," a name for the central region of India often used by Chinese Buddhist pilgrims. When translated into Chinese, it resembled the name for ancient China, Zhongguo (Middle Kingdom).

Mahayana

One of the major schools of Buddhism, usually translated as the "Great Vehicle." The school advanced the idea of the bodhisattva and stressed the involvement of laypersons in the practice of Buddhism.

Maitreya

The future Buddha, who is supposed to descend to earth at a future time to stop the turmoil and end the sufferings of the people.

Mandate of Heaven

A political idea formulated during the Zhou period of Chinese history that emphasized the role of Heaven in the downfall of an existing dynasty and the establishment of a new one. It served to legitimize the new dynasty but at the same time warned the new regime of future collapse if it failed to pay attention to the needs of the people.

Manichaeism

A Persian religion founded by the prophet Mani, who taught the duality of good and evil in cosmic and human worlds.

Manjusri

The bodhisattva of wisdom, who, according to Chinese Buddhist texts, resides on Mount Wutai in Shanxi Province, China.

Nalanda

A Buddhist institution of learning located in the present-day Bihar state of India, which attracted Buddhist and non-Buddhist students from various parts of Asia.

neo-Confucianism

Called *daoxue* or *lixue* in Chinese, this was the great flowering of Confucian thought that took place during the Song dynasty but had its roots in the latter part of the Tang dynasty, ironically (inasmuch as neo-Confucianism had absorbed a great many Buddhist tenets and practices) among anti-Buddhists such as Han Yu (768–824) but also among those who were better disposed toward Buddhism such as Li Ao (772–841).

Nestorian Christianity

Introduced to China by a Persian monk during the seventh century CE, this heretical (to Catholics and the Orthodox church) form of Christianity flourished in Central Asia and elsewhere to the east. In China, it was especially popular among Syrian merchant groups. Nestorianism essentially disappeared after the great religious persecution of 842–45, but it staged a small comeback under the Mongols during the Yuan dynasty.

nirvana

The state of nonexistence, which, according to Buddhist teachings, brings about the cessation of suffering for living creatures.

parinirvana

Literally "final nirvana," usually used to describe nirvana attained by the Sakayamuni Buddha.

Pax Romana

Literally "Roman peace," the name for the period between 27 BCE and 180 CE, when the Roman Empire was largely peaceful.

qi

Also written as *ch'i* (or *ki* in Japanese), this is the metaphysical concept of material energy that constitutes all things in the universe and may be channeled to harness power and nourish well-being.

quiet sitting

The neo-Confucian analog of Buddhist meditation.

ru

"Literati," a term that usually refers to Confucian scholar-bureaucrats.

samsara

The cycle of birth and rebirth in Buddhist teaching within which living beings reincarnate continuously based on the deeds (karma) they have performed.

sangha

The monastic community of Buddhist monks and nuns.

Shangdi

Literally "Lord on High," the name of the supreme deity in the early Chinese belief system.

Shendu

Ancient Chinese name for India.

Shibosi

The Bureau of Maritime Commerce, an office established during the Tang dynasty to oversee international maritime trade.

taiji

Figure G1

"The Great Ultimate," a cosmological concept indicating absolute and undifferentiated creativity. It is often symbolized by the *taiji tu* ("diagram of the Great Ultimate"), a circle in which there is a curved light area (*yang*) with a dark dot at its center and a curved dark area (*yin*) with a light dot at its center. The *taiji tu* first appears in Song or later times.

tianxia

Literally "[All] under Heaven," a term that essentially refers to the whole of the empire or, more vaguely and generally, the entire world. The concept embodies the notion that the ruler governs through the Mandate of Heaven.

Taiping Dao

Not to be confused with the Taiping tianguo (Taiping Rebellion, 1851–64), the enormous uprising that convulsed central and southeastern China during the mid–nineteenth century and contributed greatly to the collapse of the Qing dynasty. Taiping Dao (Way of Great Peace) was a millenarian movement that spawned a rebellion during the middle-to-late first century. *See also* Yellow Turban Rebellion and Five Pecks of Rice Daoism.

Theravada

Literally "teachings of the elders," one of the oldest schools of Buddhism, emphasizing self-awakening to the knowledge that suffering is caused by desire and that the means to end it is to follow the path of wisdom, ethical conduct, and concentration. These three aspects formed the Buddhist teaching known as the eightfold path. Wisdom indicates having the right view and intention; ethical conduct means employing right speech, action, and livelihood; and concentration highlights the right effort, right mindfulness or awareness, and right concentration or attention.

tian

"Heaven," a philosophical and religious term for the cosmos, but often contrasted with *di* ("earth") to form a sort of dualism or dyad, especially in Daoist thought. Though by no means anthropomorphic, *tian* is personified as Lao Tianye (Old [Grand]Father Heaven) among the common people.

Tianshi Dao

"Way of the Celestial Master," a Daoist movement founded by Zhang Daoling in 142 CE. It developed a theocratic state in eastern Sichuan and later split into a northern branch and a southern branch, which had influence throughout most of China. The Way of the Celestial Masters survives to this day in a number of competing lineages.

Tiantai

A Chinese Buddhist school that attempted to systematize and syncretize all Buddhist teachings that had been transmitted from India to China.

vihara

Sanskrit and Pali term for a Buddhist monastery. It originally signified "a secluded place in which to walk." In simplest terms, *vihara* were originally places for wandering monks to stay in during the rainy season.

vinaya

The rules Buddhist monks and nuns must follow.

xinxue

"Teaching of the mind," a precept and school of neo-Confucian thought that rivaled *lixue*. The chief architect and advocate of it was Wang Yangming (1472–1529).

yangban

"Two groups/ranks" of scholar-officials, the literary or civil and the military or martial. This is a term that initially appeared in the late Koryo dynasty (918–1392) in Korea and referred strictly to officeholders. During the Choson dynasty (1392–1897), starting around the sixteenth century, *yangban* came to refer more generally to both the two groups of officials and their family members, hence a privileged social class.

Yellow Turban Rebellion

A peasant rebellion near the end of the Han dynasty, named after the yellow scarves the rebels wore on their heads. Although the rebellion was eventually quelled by the Han army, the devastation and the impact were so great that they brought about the collapse of the dynasty within a few decades.

Zhongguo

Literally "Middle Kingdom," the name originally used for the region around the central Yellow River valley, and now for the modern nation of China.

NOTES

CHAPTER 1

[1] On the Confucians, see chapter 3.

[2] *Radical* refers to the core element of a Chinese character, which often conveys or is associated with the main meaning of the specific character. It usually appears on the left, top, or bottom part of a Chinese character. For example, see note 4.

[3] India in this book refers to the region that now comprises Pakistan, India, and Bangladesh.

[4] The Chinese used the term *fan* 蕃 / 番 to refer to foreigners. For some specific foreign tribes and groups they used Chinese characters with animal radicals, connoting the supposed animal-like behavior of these people. Thus the term *Di* 狄, which referred to people settled on the northern borders of China, has the dog radical, and the term *Man* 蠻, used for those in the south, has the worm or insect radical (Yang 1968: 27).

CHAPTER 2

[1] Cowries (singular *cowry* or *cowrie*) are smooth, lustrous seashells that have been used for decorative purposes and as currency for thousands of years in many parts of the world. The Chinese character for *cowry* (貝, pronounced *bei*) was originally a pictographic representation of a cowry shell. It is used as a radical in many Chinese characters related to wealth and treasure.

[2] Erlitou is located near the city of Yanshi in Henan Province. Erlitou Culture was widespread throughout the provinces of Henan, Shanxi, Shaanxi, and Hubei.

[3] The Caucasus is a mountainous region situated between the Black and Caspian seas at the strategic nexus between Europe, Asia, and the Middle East.

CHAPTER 3

[1] Xiongnu is the Modern Standard Mandarin pronunciation of the Old Sinitic transcription of the name Hun, although this does not mean that the Xiongnu who made incursions into China during the Qin and Han were the same people as the Huns who invaded Europe from the east centuries later.

[2] The "Roof of the World," the Pamir Mountains, are formed by the junction of the Tian Shan (Heavenly Mountains) in eastern Central Asia and the Karakorum, Kunlun, and Hindu Kush ranges. The Pamirs divide eastern from western Central Asia.

[3] The Taklamakan is one of the largest and harshest deserts in the world. It fills the Tarim Basin, in the southern part of eastern Central Asia.

[4] Bactria was located between the Hindu Kush mountains and the Amu Darya (Oxus River).

[5] The Zoroastrian idea of duality refers to a system of belief that posits two opposing forces, in this case good and evil.

CHAPTER 4

[1] This scholarly debate about the early transmission of Buddhism to China continues without any conclusion. It is possible that Buddhist ideas were initially transmitted via both overland and maritime routes.

CHAPTER 5

[1] A catty is equal to about 1.5 pounds, a tael is equal to 40 grams of silver, and a bolt of fabric is equal to 40 yards.

APPENDIX

[1] *Chi* is roughly a foot; *zhang* is around ten feet; *fen* is equal to 3.3 mm; and *qian* is about 5 grams.

Bibliography and Suggestions for Further Reading

Abramson, Marc S. 2008. *Ethnic Identity in Tang China*. Philadelphia: University of Pennsylvania Press.

Adshead, S. A. M. 2000. *China in World History*. 3rd ed. New York: St. Martin's Press.

———. 2004. *T'ang China: The Rise of the East in World History*. New York: Palgrave Macmillan.

Ahmed, S. Maqbul. 1989. *Arabic Classical Accounts of India and China*. Calcutta: Indian Institute of Advanced Studies.

Bentley, Jerry H. 1993. *Old World Encounters: Cross-Cultural Contacts and Exchanges in Pre-modern Times*. Oxford: Oxford University Press.

Ch'en, Kenneth. 1964. *Buddhism in China: A Historical Survey*. Princeton: Princeton University Press.

Cohen, Warren I. 2000. *East Asia at the Center: Four Thousand Years of Engagement with the World*. New York: Columbia University Press.

Di Cosmo, Nicola. 2002. *Ancient China and Its Enemies: The Rise of Nomadic Power in East Asian History*. Cambridge: Cambridge University Press.

Dreyer, Edward L. 2006. *Zheng He: China and the Oceans in the Early Ming Dynasty, 1405–1433*. New York: Pearson Longman.

Fairbank, John K. 1968. *The Chinese World Order: Traditional China's Foreign Relations*. Cambridge: Harvard University Press.

Foltz, Richard C. 1999. *Religions of the Silk Road: Overland Trade and Cultural Exchange from Antiquity to the Fifteenth Century*. New York: St. Martin's Press.

Golden, Peter B. 2011. *Central Asia in World History*. New York: Oxford University Press.

Goodrich, Chauncey. 1984. "Riding Astride and the Saddle in Ancient China." *Harvard Journal of Asiatic Studies* 44.2: 279–306.

Gordon, Stewart. 2008. *When Asia Was the World: Traveling Merchants, Scholars, Warriors, and Monks Who Created the "Riches of the East."* Philadelphia: Da Capo Press.

Hansen, Valerie. 2000. *The Open Empire: A History of China to 1600.* New York: W. W. Norton.

Higham, Charles. 1996. *The Bronze Age of Southeast Asia.* Cambridge: Cambridge University Press.

Hirth, Friedrich, and W. W. Rockhill. [1911] 1966. *Chau Ju-kua: His Work on the Chinese and Arab Trade in the Twelfth and Thirteenth Centuries, Entitled Chu-fan-chi.* Saint Petersburg: Printing Office of the Imperial Academy of Sciences; rpt.

Holcombe, Charles. 2001. *The Genesis of East Asia, 221 B.C.–A.D. 907.* Honolulu: University of Hawai'i Press.

Karashima, Noboru, and Tansen Sen. 2009. "Chinese Texts Describing or Referring to the Chola Kingdom as Zhu-nian." In *Nagapattinam to Suvarnadwipa: Reflections on the Chola Naval Expeditions to Southeast Asia,* edited by Hermann Kulke, K. Kesavapany, and Vijay Sakhuja, 292–315. Singapore: Institute of Southeast Asian Studies.

Keates, S. G. 2004. "Home Range Size in Middle Pleistocene China and Human Dispersal Patterns in Eastern and Central Asia." *Asian Perspectives* 43.2: 227–47.

Kuzmina, E. E. 2008. *The Prehistory of the Silk Road.* Philadelphia: University of Pennsylvania Press.

Legge, James. [1886] 1965. *A Record of Buddhistic Kingdoms.* New York: Paragon Book.

Levathes, Louise. 1994. *When China Ruled the Seas: The Treasure Fleet of the Dragon Throne, 1405–1433.* New York: Simon and Schuster.

Lewis, Mark Edward. 2009. *China's Cosmopolitan Empire: The Tang Dynasty.* Cambridge: Belknap Press of Harvard University Press.

Li, Qingxin. 2006. *Maritime Silk Road.* Beijing: China Intercontinental Press.

Li, Rongxi, tr. 1995. *A Biography of the Tripitaka Master of the Great Ci'en Monastery of the Great Tang Dynasty*. Berkeley: Numata Center for Buddhist Translation and Research.

————, tr. 2002. "The Journey of the Eminent Monk Faxian." In *Lives of Great Monks and Nuns*, BDK English Tripitaka, 155–214. Berkeley: Numata Center for Buddhist Translation and Research.

Li, Y. 2006. "On the Function of Cowries in Shang and Western Zhou China." *Journal of East Asian Archeology* 5: 1–26.

Lieberman, Victor. 2003–10. *Strange Parallels: Southeast Asia in Global Context, c. 800–1830.* 2 vols. Cambridge: Cambridge University Press.

Liu, Li. 2004. *The Chinese Neolithic: Trajectories to Early States*. Cambridge: Cambridge University Press.

Liu, Xinru. 1988. *Ancient India and Ancient China: Trade and Religious Exchanges, AD 1–600*. Delhi: Oxford University Press.

————. 2010. *The Silk Road in World History*. New York: Oxford University Press.

Liu, Xinru, and Lynda Norene Shaffer. 2007. *Connections across Eurasia: Transportation, Communication, and Cultural Exchange on the Silk Roads*. New York: McGraw-Hill.

Mair, Victor H. 2005. "The North(west)ern Peoples and the Recurrent Origins of the 'Chinese' State." In *The Teleology of the Modern Nation-State: Japan and China*, edited by Joshua A. Fogel, 46–86. Philadelphia: University of Pennsylvania Press.

————, ed. 2006. *Contact and Exchange in the Ancient World*. Honolulu: University of Hawai'i Press.

————, tr. and intro. 2007. *The Art of War: Sun Zi's Military Methods*. New York: Columbia University Press.

Mallory, J. P. 1991. *In Search of the Indo-Europeans: Language, Archaeology, and Myth*. London: Thames and Hudson.

Mallory, J. P., and Victor H. Mair. 2000. *The Tarim Mummies: Ancient China and the Mystery of the Earliest Peoples from the West*. London: Thames and Hudson.

Mei, J. 2000. *Copper and Bronze Metallurgy in Late Prehistoric Xinjiang: Its Cultural Context and Relationship with Neighboring Regions*. Oxford: Archeopress.

Mei, Jianjun, and Thilo Rehren, eds. 2009. *Metallurgy and Civilisation: Eurasia and Beyond*. London: Archetype.

Mills, J. V. G., tr. [1970] 1997. *Ma Huan Ying-yai sheng-lan: "The Overall Survey of the Ocean's Shores" {1433}*. Bangkok: White Lotus Press.

Pan, Yihong. 1997. *Song of Heaven and Heavenly Qaghan: Sui-Tang China and Its Neighbors*. Bellington: Western Washington University Press.

Pirazzoli-t'Serstevens, M. 1992. "Cowry and Chinese Copper Cash as Prestige Goods in Dian." In *Southeast Asian Archaeology, 1990*, edited by I. C. Glover, 45–52. Hull: Centre for South-East Asian Studies, University of Hull.

Ropp, Paul S. 2010. *China in World History*. New York: Oxford University Press.

Rossabi, Morris. 1983. *China among Equals: The Middle Kingdom and Its Neighbors, 10th–14th Centuries*. Berkeley: University of California Press.

Rothschild, N. Harry. 2007. *Wu Zhao: China's Only Female Emperor*. Harlow: Longman.

Schafer, Edward H. 1963. *The Golden Peaches of Samarkand: A Study of T'ang Exotics*. Berkeley: University of California Press.

Sen, Tansen. 2003. *Buddhism, Diplomacy, and Trade: The Realignment of Sino-Indian Relations, 600–1400*. Honolulu: University of Hawai'i Press.

———. 2006. "The Travel Records of Chinese Pilgrims, Faxian, Xuanzang, and Yijing: Sources for the Cross-Cultural Encounters between Ancient China and Ancient India." *Education about Asia* 11.3 (winter): 24–33.

Shaughnessy, Edward L. 1988. "Historical Perspectives on the Introduction of the Chariot into China." *Harvard Journal of Asiatic Studies* 48.1 (June): 189–237.

Solheim, W. G. 2000. "Taiwan, Coastal South China, and Northern Viet Nam and the Nusantao Maritime Trading Network." *Journal of East Asian Archaeology*. 2.1–2: 273–84.

Thorp, Robert L. 2006. *China in the Early Bronze Age: Shang Civilization.* Philadelphia: University of Pennsylvania Press.

Tsunoda, Ryusaku, and William Theodore de Bary, eds. 1964. *Sources of Japanese Tradition.* New York: Columbia University Press.

Vogel, Hans Ulrich. 1993a. "Cowry Trade and Its Role in the Economy of Yunnan: From the Ninth to the Mid-Seventeenth Century (Part I)." *Journal of the Economic and Social History of the Orient* 36.3: 211–52.

———. 1993b. "Cowry Trade and Its Role in the Economy of Yunnan: From the Ninth to the Mid-Seventeenth Century (Part II)." *Journal of the Economic and Social History of the Orient* 36.4: 309–53.

Waley-Cohen, Joanna. 1999. *The Sextants of Beijing: Global Currents in Chinese History.* New York: W. W. Norton.

Wang, Gungwu. 1958. "The Nanhai Trade: A Study of the Early History of Chinese Trade in the South China Sea." *Journal of the Malayan Branch of the Royal Asiatic Society* 31.2: 1–135.

Wang, Zhenping. 1994. "Speaking with a Forked Tongue: Sino-Japanese Diplomatic Correspondence, 238–608." *Journal of the American Oriental Society* 114.1: 23–32.

———. 2005. *Ambassadors from the Island of Immortals: China-Japan Relations in the Han-Tang Period.* Honolulu: University of Hawai'i Press.

Watson, Burton, tr. [1961] 1993. *Records of the Grand Historian: Han Dynasty II.* Rev. ed. Hong Kong and New York: Chinese University of Hong Kong and Columbia University Press.

White, Joyce C., and Elizabeth G. Hamilton. 2010. "The Transmission of Early Bronze Technology to Thailand: New Perspectives." *Journal of World Prehistory* 22.4: 357–97.

Whitfield, Susan. 1999. *Life along the Silk Road.* Berkeley: University of California Press.

Wriggins, Sally Hovey. 2004. *The Silk Road Journey with Xuanzang.* Boulder: Westview Press.

Wu, Hung. 1986. "Buddhist Elements in Early Chinese Art (2nd and 3rd Centuries A.D.)." *Artibus Asiae* 47.3–4: 263–316.

Wu Zhuanjun, ed. 2008. *Haishang Sichou zhi lu yanjiu* [Research on the Maritime Silk Route]. Beijing: Kexue chubanshe.

Yang, Bin. 2009. *Between Winds and Clouds: The Making of Yunnan (Second Century BCE to Twentieth Century CE)*. New York: Columbia University Press.

Yang, Lien-sheng. 1968. "Historical Notes on the Chinese World Order." In *The Chinese World Order: Traditional China's Foreign Relations*, edited by John King Fairbank, 20–33. Cambridge: Harvard University Press.

Yu, Taishan. 1998. "A Study of Saka History." *Sino-Platonic Papers* 80 (July): 1–225.

Yu, Ying-shih. 1967. *Trade and Expansion in Han China: A Study in the Structure of Sino-Barbarian Economic Relations*. Berkeley: University of California Press.

CPSIA information can be obtained
at www.ICGtesting.com
Printed in the USA
JSHW042332191021
19679JS00001B/4